WESTMAR COLLEGE LIBRARY

W9-BPS-547

THE U.S. INTELLIGENCE COMMUNITY

Stafford T. Thomas

UNIVERSITY
PRESS OF
AMERICA

LANHAM • NEW YORK • LONDON

JK
468
.I6
T46
1983

Copyright © 1983 by

University Press of America,™ Inc.

4720 Boston Way
Lanham, MD 20706

3 Henrietta Street
London WC2E 8LU England

All rights reserved

Printed in the United States of America

Library of Congress Cataloging in Publication Data

Thomas, Stafford T., 1941–
    The U.S. intelligence community.

    Bibliography: p.
    1. Intelligence Service—United States. 2. United States.
Central Intelligence Agency. I. Title.
JK468.I6T46   1983   327.1'2'0973   83–1246
ISBN 0–8191–3098–2
ISBN 0–8191–3099–0 (pbk.)

103144

DEDICATION

For my parents

and

For C.B.

My Best Friend

ACKNOWLEDGEMENTS

I would like to thank those who have provided me with support and encouragement in writing this book. My academic mentors, especially Manus Midlarsky and the late Ben Burnett, did their best to teach me how to be objective and intellectually honest and curious. My students and colleagues have offered countless suggestions that have helped me in conceiving the different aspects of this subject. Ray Cline and Harry Howe Ransom have been particularly important in encouraging me to pursue the subject in an academic and scholastic manner. The secretarial pool at Canisius College managed to interpret my handwriting and produce a draft manuscript. Linda Duby, Carolyn McCants, and my wonderful wife Carol Berg typed the succeeding drafts, including this final copy. All of these people were indispensable, but my special and eternal thanks go to my wife and son who were tolerant, patient, and supportive and who served as my chief editors, critics, and inspirations. Without them, this work would not be.

TABLE OF CONTENTS

PREFACE

The purpose of this book is to introduce you to the U.S. Intelligence Community. The typical perspective of the community is dominated by the CIA and especially its more glamorous and mysterious activities. That perspective is not totally false, but is so distorted that it needs correcting. My assumption is that you want to learn about the intelligence community, what it really is like, what it really does, why it performs and fails to perform, and what difference it makes.

I have tried to maintain an objectivity in dealing with a phenomenon that is highly subjective. Since I have never worked for or in the community, I have no biases resulting from previous employment. This objectivity is important in achieving an understanding of the material and is critical in presenting the problems of the community. The significance of this objectivity is that it permits the investigation of intelligence phenomena using the same methodological criteria and theoretical considerations that are applied in other areas of political and social science.

The material is inherently the object of debate. This debate has two basic aspects. The more common focus of the debate concerns the propriety of the operations of the intelligence community, especially on behalf of a free, democratic society. The other main aspect of the debate concerns the utility of the intelligence community and its contributions to national security and foreign policy. I have concentrated on the second question, although Chapter 5 discusses the problem of secrecy in an open society.

The purpose of this book is to describe the intelligence community and to indicate some of the major issues and problems connected with the production of intelligence and the conduct of operations. I hope that it achieves its basic goal, to enhance the objective assessment of the U.S. Intelligence Community.

CHAPTER 1

What Do We Mean By "Intelligence?"

Introduction

There is an aura that surrounds the work and activity of the intelligence community, the aura of "cloak and dagger." When most people hear of or read about the CIA, the KGB, or any other intelligence organization, the usual image is of handsome spies chasing master international criminals with the assistance of beautiful women. Another version of the popular understanding of "intelligence" is the patient counterespionage agent working to uncover the "mole" planted by the opposition's secret service to report on plans and operations directed against that enemy. Such drama does occasionally characterize espionage, and certainly such tedium is a fact of the counterintelligence process, but these interpretations of "intelligence" are misleading and inaccurate. The public attraction to the dangerous and sensational aspects of intelligence work ignores the majority of intelligence activity and even distorts the clandestine operations that are the subjects of most popular "spy" fiction. Therefore, before we examine the intelligence community, it is imperative that we define our subject.

Serious and objective investigation of national intelligence is a fairly recent phenomenon. While there are classic treatises on the importance of intelligence to policy making and implementation, the subject has not been a major concern to scholars until recently.[1] The field has been dominated by fiction writers who have understandably focused on the daring exploits of secret agents. The result has been a lack of appreciation for the essence of intelligence work, compounded by a misunderstanding of what "intelligence" means. This book is intended to provide an introduction to the U.S. intelligence community as a part of American national government and the policy making process.

The Organization of the Book

Each chapter addresses a different aspect of the community in order to accomplish three goals. One is to inform the student about the intelligence community, its background, components, activities, rationale, and problems. Knowledge of these primarily descriptive features of the subject is the minimum requirement if one wants to think about or discuss the topic of intelligence intelligently. A second theme of the book is to apply various theories, ideas, and models of related academic subjects that can be used to gain a better understanding of why the community does what it does and why it fails to do what some expect it to do. This analytical aspect of the book is intended to suggest explanations and arouse the intellectual curiosity of the student. Finally, the book addresses the inherent problems of the intelligence community. Some of these problems are similar in form to those of other governmental bureaucracies, departments, and agencies. But the intelligence community is characterized by unique features that make most of its problems into dilemmas. These parts of the book present the problems without suggesting definitive solutions in order to provoke discussion and debate. It is only through such discussion and debate that further progress toward greater knowledge of the intelligence community can be achieved.

Chapter 2 provides an historical perspective, emphasizing the direct relationship between an active, vibrant intelligence apparatus and the perception of a threatening environment to the United States. The most extreme threat (actual as well as perceived) to U.S. national security was World War II, and beginning with our involvement in that war, the environment has continued to contain threatening aspects. Consequently, a major intelligence effort was mounted in World War II and intelligence continues to be an important and usually vital part of policy making.

Chapter 3 describes the various structures of the U.S. intelligence community together with the intelligence functions they perform, although little attention is paid to the CIA, which is the subject of Chapter 4. Except for the CIA, most of the intelligence community is unknown to most people. However, other members of the community are larger than the CIA, have a bigger budget than the CIA, contribute critical intelligence that cannot be obtained by the CIA, and successfully contradict CIA intelligence estimates and policy advice. Basic knowledge of the entire community is fundamental to an understanding of the scope of intelligence concerns, capabilities, and even limitations.

The Central Intelligence Agency is the focus of Chapter 4. The CIA is the community component that most people recognize, and its activities have been the subject of intense scrutiny, debate, and emotions. Most people associate only espionage (spying) and covert activity (especially paramilitary ventures) with the CIA. This chapter illustrates that the duties and functions of the CIA include a number of different activities, some of which are far more relevant to policy making than the "cloak and dagger" operations of popular fiction.

Chapters 5, 6, and 7 present some of the most crucial problems of the intelligence community. In Chapter 5, the major internal problems are discussed, especially the difficulty of achieving coordination among the diverse elements of the community. Chapter 6 focuses on the problems reflected in the domestic environment of the community, emphasizing the question of the proper role of a secret governmental organization in a free and representative society. Chapter 7 addresses the foreign problems, including relations with both allies and adversaries, chief of which is the Soviet KGB. These chapters are not intended to solve these various problems, but rather to acquaint the student with the nature and substance of the problems.

An Appendix is included that illustrates how an espionage network (a reseau to "insiders") is organized and operated. While it is of less academic concern than the rest of the book, this material indicates that successful espionage is more a matter of proper management techniques and application of principles of psychology than a result of serendipity and drama.

What is "Intelligence?"

In dealing with this somewhat mystical and arcane subject in an academic manner, it is critical that useful and accurate definitions be given to the basic concepts in the field. This need for greater conceptual clarity is most evident in the several meanings that the term "intelligence" has. Much of the misunderstanding and distortion that characterizes the observations about the intelligence community results from failure to use the term "intelligence" appropriately.[2]

There are three major interpretations of the term "intelligence" that are relevant to the "intelligence community." One of these refers to the various products generated by the community. A second definition concerns the process that characterizes community functions. A third definition of "intelligence" means the clandestine operations that are the subject of the bulk of the popular literature.

Product.[3] "Intelligence" often is used to denote the products that are prepared and distributed by the intelligence community. There is a great deal of variety among these products, but all of them share a common goal, to provide information that is useful for the purposes of making and executing policy, especially national security policy and foreign policy.[4]

Some of these products are generated periodically, while others are done on an ad hoc basis. The periodic products include daily, weekly, monthly, and annual reports that update items of interest to the various consumers of intelligence. For instance, the President is given a review of world crises every day which serves to alert him to situations of actual or potential concern. This Daily Intelligence Report is usually succinct and normally contains no analysis. It is a distillation of important world events, compiled overnight by the intelligence community and produced by the CIA's Office of Current Intelligence. A

3

modified edition of this product is distributed throughout the intelligence community and to other parts of the government, although its circulation is limited, based on the position and security clearance of the recipients.

Other periodic reports focus on specific problems or concerns. The subjects of these reports are very extensive. These products include such diverse topics as Soviet missile capabilities, the number, locations, and tactics of terrorists, regional production of foodstuffs and raw materials, changes in governments around the world, purchases of armaments, and international economic and financial activities. The frequency of these products varies, as does the clientele who receive them. Also, some of these products are "straight" reports of factual material, while others contain extensive analysis and predictions. All of them serve to inform policy makers, although few explicitly prescribe definitive courses of actions.

Non-periodic products are either generated in response to a specific request or produced by the intelligence community's analysts because they recognize the product's importance. This intelligence is often highly important, since it usually implies some kind of crisis decision. The President may require information on a terrorist group holding hostages, the Secretary of Defense may need to know the military posture of a Middle East country, or community analysts may have concluded that a <u>coup d'etat</u> is imminent in some Third World country. Because the United States is a world power whose interests are global and continual, American policy makers must necessarily be kept informed and the intelligence products are intended to provide this information.

The most important intelligence product is the National Intelligence Estimate (NIE).[5] These are produced on both a periodic and non-periodic basis, and they deal with a variety of subjects. The primary NIE consumer is the President, although many people usually receive them and occasionally they are declassified and made public. NIEs often represent the collective judgement of the intelligence community, which means they reflect compromise among the various community structures. Other National Intelligence Estimates are prepared by individual analysts and are similar to academic papers in style and methodological rigor. Different presidents have viewed the utility of NIEs to policy deliberations in different ways. A dilemma for the intelligence community is that a product that is objective and non-prescriptive is often viewed as unsatisfactory by a President who often is partisan and in need of advice. A related problem in the production of intelligence is that coordinating the various community members is an extremely difficult task. These problems are examined in greater detail in Chapters 3 and 5.

4

Process.[6] The process by which "intelligence" is produced involves several steps that are conceptually distinct as separate functions, but which overlap in reality.[7] The process begins with the collection of information and concludes with the distribution of the product to the relevant consumer(s). The effect of the process is to transform individual bits and pieces of data into a product that decision makers can use to help choose from among several policy options. The intermediate steps in the intelligence process are the evaluation of the accuracy, authenticity, and reliability of the collected information, the integration of various data into some kind of interrelated pattern, the analysis of the resulting pattern of information based on other known and suspected or hypothesized patterns, and the interpretation of the emerging intelligence in terms of projections into the future.

The task of producing intelligence emphasizes academic skills such as methodological training, objective consideration of the conclusions, and continual reevaluation of assumptions by the analyst. Consequently, most intelligence producers have advanced academic degrees and are temperamentally and vocationally removed from the ethos of the "secret agent." These analysts rely on "open" sources of data even more than "closed" sources, although the latter may provide critical information that substantially affects the intelligence product.

There is an obvious relationship between the intelligence-as-product and intelligence-as-process definitions. However, the two meanings are distinctly different and awareness of the difference permits a clearer understanding of the work of the intelligence community. Neither of these definitions relates to the usual interpretation of intelligence, that of espionage, counterespionage, and covert action.

Clandestine Service.[8] This meaning implies operations of a secret nature. The three basic types of clandestine service (the term by which the CIA's Directorate of Operations is commonly known) are espionage, counterespionage, and covert action. These activities are discussed in greater detail in Chapters 4 and 7, and espionage is the subject of the Appendix. Basically, espionage is intended to collect information, counterespionage is intended to protect U.S. espionage efforts and to collect information on the espionage efforts of adversaries, and covert actions are intended to influence policies and situations in other countries. Covert actions in particular have been the subject of recent debate in America, and this debate is the main focus of Chapter 6.

The range of past foreign covert action operations has been extensive and has included secret support for propaganda efforts, funding political parties of various perspectives and places on the political spectrum, running institutes for media representatives to instruct them in reporting techniques in both open and closed societies, organizing and supervising the overthrow of regimes, financing and prosecuting guerrilla wars, and attempted assassinations of foreign leaders. In virtually all of these covert actions, the authorization has come from the President and his foreign policy advisors. The responsibility for implementing these operations has usually rested with the CIA's Directorate of Operations, previously known as the Office of Policy Coordination and the Directorate of Plans.

Conclusion

Covert action and other clandestine services are the most commonly known activities of the intelligence community. The product and process definitions of "intelligence" are neither glamorous nor dramatic. However, they are indispensable to effective decision making, and they are far less controversial since they are accepted as necessary ingredients in the policy process. Despite this wide acceptance, the importance of an intelligence community has not always been viewed as necessary or vital in U.S. history.

NOTES

1. The first "classic" treatment of the subject was by the Chinese historian and strategist Sun Tzu, whose life, intersts, and thoughts are remarkably similar to Machiavelli's. Sun Tzu on the Art of War (New York: Oxford University Press, 1963). Also see Francis Dvornik, Origins of Intelligence Services (New Brunswick, NJ: Rutgers University Press, 1974).

2. This general need for greater conceptual clarity in the scholarly investigation of intelligence is the theme of Harry Howe Ransom's "Strategic Intelligence and Foreign Policy," World Politics, 27 (October 1974).

3. Sherman Kent, Strategic Intelligence for American World Power (Princeton, NJ: Princeton University Press, 1966), Harry Howe Ransom, "Intelligence: Political and Military," International Encyclopedia of the Social Sciences (New York: Crowell, Collier and Macmillan, Inc., 1968), and Roy Godson, ed., Intelligence Requirements for the 1980's: Analysis and Estimates (Washington: National Strategy Information Center, Inc., 1980).

4. Kent classifies intelligence products as descriptive, reportorial, speculative-evaluative, tactical/operational, and counterintelligence/espionage. Kent, op. cit.

5. Harry Howe Ransom, The Intelligence Establishment (Cambridge, MA: Harvard University Press, 1970), Ray Cline, Secrets, Spies and Scholars: Blueprint of the Essential CIA (Washington: Acropolis Books, 1976), and Lawrence Freedman, U. S. Intelligence and the Soviet Strategic Threat (Boulder, CO: Westview Press, 1977).

6. Allen Dulles, The Craft of Intelligence (New York: Harper and Row Publishers, 1963) and Kent, op. cit., Part III.

7. Stafford T. Thomas, "On the Selection of Directors of Central Intelligence," Southeastern Political Review, 9 (Spring 1981), Lyman B. Kirkpatrick, Jr., The U. S. Intelligence Community: Foreign Policy and Domestic Activities (New York: Hill and Wang, 1973), Ransom, The Intelligence Establishment, Dictionary of United States Military Terms for Joint Usage (Washington: Departments of the Army, Navy, and Air Force, 1955), and Washington Platt, Strategic Intelligence Production: Basic Principles (New York: Praeger, 1957).

8. Roy Godson, ed., Intelligence Requirements for the 1980's: Elements of Intelligence (Washington: National Strategy Information Center, Inc., 1979).

CHAPTER 2

The History of the U.S. Intelligence Community[1]

The most significant factor in the historical development of the intelligence community has been the involvement of the United States in wars or threats of war. Beginning with the Revolutionary War, the salience of the intelligence service has been determined by the role we have played in world affairs. The more acute the crisis or threat, the more important intelligence has become to our national security.[2] In times of peace when we were fortunate to not be threatened by other countries, intelligence has naturally been less important because it was not required by our policy makers.

During the Revolutionary War, our military leaders required considerable intelligence on British troop movements and plans. Also, because the British were actively trying to know about our troop movements and plans, it was vital that we protect our secrets. This was our first major venture into the world of espionage and counterespionage. It introduced us to one of the games of international relations that most other contemporary countries had been playing for centuries. As newcomers to this game, we did surprisingly well. Our victory in the war cannot be attributed solely to superior intelligence, but neither did our lack of experience result in any great disasters.[3]

The Revolutionary War did produce two names to the folklore of American history. These two men have become symbols for treason and patriotism. The traitor was Benedict Arnold. A general in the Continental Army, Arnold was an extremely competent and important member of George Washington's effort against the British. Arnold was given the responsibility of organizing and implementing the defense of West Point on the Hudson River in New York. West Point, which became the site for the U.S. Military Academy in 1802, was a fortress that hindered British strategy, and as such it was of vital importance to the Americans. Arnold conspired to sell the plans for West Point's fortifications to the British. His intentions were discovered and, while he escaped to live out a nondescript life in England, the British were unable to capitalize on their acquired intelligence. Benedict Arnold was the earliest important traitor in American history and his name has always been associated with treason.[4]

In contrast to Arnold, Nathan Hale became our first espionage hero. Hale led a group of soldiers in what amounted to a guerrilla campaign against the British. Because of this method of fighting, he was able to acquire information on British plans. While this information was of only marginal utility, Hale's patriotic fervor has made him an intelligence hero. He was captured by the British and executed as a spy. While his reputed last words about regret that he had but one life to give for his country may be folklore, he remains an important symbol of the dedication current intelligence officers have.[5] Indeed, in the rotunda of the CIA headquarters building in Langley, Virginia is a larger-than-lifesize statue of Nathan Hale with his memorable epitaph inscribed.

Following the Revolutionary War, the United States began a practice that was to be repeated until World War II. In times of peace the intelligence community suffered from neglect and disrespect. When crises threatened or war broke out, intelligence became an important part of our national security policy. This vacillating attitude toward intelligence was partly due to a distrust of secrecy and a desire for an open government answerable to the people. These were among the principles fought for during the Revolution and debated at the Continental Congress. It would be naive to suggest that our government was ever totally open or answerable to the people, but the idea of a secret governmental organization was considered inconsistent with democracy and representative government. Thus, one reason for a decline in intelligence following the Revolutionary War (and subsequent ones) was philosophical.

A second reason why intelligence was neglected in periods of peace was more practical. The policy makers did not require a great deal of intelligence because the United States was pursuing a policy of political isolation. The primary themes of U.S. policy in the 19th century were continental expansion and hemispheric hegemony. Our goal was to dominate the Western Hemisphere, both laterally by pushing our frontiers to the Pacific Ocean (and beyond) and longitudinally by invoking the Monroe Doctrine to prevent further colonization by European powers and by encouraging revolutions throughout Latin America to gain independence for erstwhile colonies. By a combination of good fortune and some skilled diplomacy, we were able to achieve these goals without the resort to major or prolonged wars with other nations. With a few minor exceptions, we were not challenged or threatened by other powerful countries. Thus, our foreign concerns did not require a great deal of intelligence and our resources were allocated in other areas.

There were short periods when intelligence was necessary, but these were brief and focused on military concerns.[6] Naturally, there was a great deal of intelligence activity during the Civil War, as each side spied extensively on the other.[7] Throughout the 19th century, most of our organized intelligence activity was conducted out of the Departments of War and Navy, although some other channels were used. We received some information from commercial enterprises, especially in Latin America, and the State Department provided sporadic diplomatic intelligence. Generally, however, our intelligence activities were haphazard and uncoordinated. This may seem deplorable, but it was probably inevitable since our needs (real as well as perceived) did not require any ongoing strong commitment to intelligence. Indeed, in April, 1917, Army Intelligence consisted of four individuals and reflected the attitude that intelligence was a branch of military service that was a repository of incompetents who were undergoing career punishment or exile.

During our military involvement in World War I, our intelligence needs rose dramatically. Those needs were almost exclusively military and were focused on the war effort. Little consideration was given to post-war intelligence needs. In fact, President Wilson's Fourteen Points indicated that covert activity would be inconsistent with American ideals. The result was a severe retrenchment of intelligence activity following the armistice. The historical and traditional pattern was continued. The U.S. return to isolationism, vividly manifested by the rejection of the League of Nations, reflected a spirit of idealism that could in no way include spying on other nations. This attitude was summarized by Secretary of State Henry L. Stimson who closed the State Department code section on the grounds that "Gentlemen do not read each other's mail."[8]

This neglect of the intelligence function continued to characterize U.S. policy throughout the 1930s. The euphoria of idealism that victory in World War I produced, the desire to remain isolated from and neutral toward European politics, and the exigencies of the Depression combined to preempt the idea of having extensive knowledge of external world events. However, by 1941, it was evident that knowledge was necessary, and President Roosevelt determined that we should begin to organize some sort of apparatus to acquire the intelligence we needed. He directed General William J. Donovan to begin discussions with Britain's secret service representative to the U.S., William Stephenson, and instructed Donovan to organize an intelligence unit for the American government.[9]

Roosevelt's decision to begin peacetime intelligence work resulted in the creation of the Office of Coordination and Information (OCI) on July 11, 1941.[10] This date is important because since that time America has not been without some sort of intelligence community. Except for a brief period following World War II, that community has been a key element of our foreign and national security policy. The creation of OCI, which became the Office of Strategic Services (OSS) in June of 1942, ended the pattern of sporadic and tentative involvement in intelligence. However, creation of a coordinating body did not immediately result in a coordinated intelligence effort.

11

The Japanese attack on Pearl Harbor has been characterized as our first great "intelligence failure."[11] It indicates the distinction between information and intelligence. All of the critical information regarding the attack was known to the U.S. government, but it remained information because it had not been processed into intelligence. The Japanese code had been broken in the summer of 1941, and the State Department was privy to all of the diplomatic cables between Tokyo and the Japanese representatives in Washington. Also, the Navy and War Departments were aware of Japanese military activities, including the westward sailing of a large task force of aircraft carriers in late November of 1941. Thus, the collection of information was excellent. The evaluation, integration, and analysis of the information was nearly nonexistent, and the dissemination of even "raw" information was haphazard, and the result was total surprise on December 7. This intelligence failure was monumental, and reaction to Pearl Harbor created a climate in which intelligence was viewed as vital to the war effort. While U.S. intelligence efforts during World War II would undoubtedly have been great anyway, the realization that we could have been forewarned about the Japanese attack resulted in a commitment to the idea of an intelligence organization that would continue following our war victory. Thus, the beginning of an established, institutionalized intelligence community had its true beginnings with the Office of Strategic Services.

The OSS began as a small group of men and women whose primary task was the production of intelligence. Because the United States had been relatively unconcerned with much of the world, there was an urgent need to obtain any information which may prove useful to our war effort. The early days of OSS emphasized this collection function. OSS people engaged in extensive research on well-known as well as remote and obscure phenomena. The enemy (Germany, Italy, and Japan, plus their allies) were of special importance, but efforts were not limited to them. The scope of OSS interest was virtually unlimited and included nations and other political groupings (such as governments-in-exile) and functional considerations (such as beach sand gradients, weather patterns, and natural resource locations). From its small beginnings and because of its broad range of pursuits, the Office of Strategic Services grew to a sizable bureaucracy. By the end of the war its payroll exceeded 13,000, of whom 5,500 worked in Washington D.C. The nature of its work meant that many of its employees were "high grade" personnel in terms of education and social status. With its rapid expansion, it became a complex bureaucracy, performing a variety of tasks. Although it lasted just over three years (June 1942-October 1945), it demonstrated the crucial contribution an intelligence service could make to American postwar foreign policy.[12]

The OSS presaged the postwar intelligence community in three main ways. It began as a part of the Executive Office of the President, which gave it high-level credentials and a degree of immunity and strength in the inevitable bureaucratic struggles with rival agencies and departments. However, it was not completely autonomous, since some of its overseas operations were under the control of local U.S. military commanders. The result was ambiguity in the authority and responsibility for its activities. In some cases, especially the production of intelligence and certain espionage activities, the OSS was autonomous in defining its objectives and determining the appropriate ways of achieving those objectives. In other instances, the OSS operated as an extension of the military effort directed by the Departments of War and Navy. In the former case it encountered hostility from established structures of the U.S. government who resented the creation of a new agency. This hostility was especially manifest in the military services, which felt their respective intelligence units were capable of assuming the burdens of wartime demands, and in the State Department, which was anxious to engage in "civilian" intelligence and resented the use of State Department "cover" for individuals who did not work for it. These early domestic bureaucratic struggles continue to characterize the intelligence community, as we will see.

A second aspect of the OSS that continues to characterize contemporary U.S. intelligence was its involvement in covert operations.[13] These activities differ from the production of intelligence, since they involve the use of the intelligence organization in a direct, active way. The collection of information, its processing into intelligence, and the dissemination of that intelligence to appropriate decision makers is a passive foreign policy exercise that serves as an input to policy making. Covert operations are the enactment of policy implementation. The production of intelligence from information involves a completely different set of priorities, values, and considerations from covert operations. Covert operations were added to the list of OSS functions after its intelligence mission was an accepted feature of American government. Due to the military priorities of World War II, there was little debate or disagreement that the United States should be involved in any activity to shorten the war and defeat the enemy. The conceptual and actual distinction between producing intelligence and using that intelligence to plan on one hand and executing operations against the enemy on the other was obscured by the single goal of winning the war. So, covert operations became a part of the intelligence community by default and were accepted as a function to be performed by the CIA and the other members of the postwar intelligence apparatus. The potential incompatibility of these two functions was not considered a fundamental issue at the time they were joined, and they continue to be performed by the same organizations today, although

13

the debate over the propriety and utility of this union has now become a quite vocal one.

The third way in which the OSS contributed to the postwar intelligence community was in its internal organization.[14] The OSS was our first major intelligence service. Its rapid and extensive growth resulted in a number of structures which are manifest in the current CIA. Chart 2.1 shows the major parts of the OSS.

The General Counsel was responsible for providing administrative coordination and legal representation, establishing and maintaining "cover" corporations (media, transportation, etc.), and making foreign and domestic contracts. Of special importance to the General Counsel was the principle of unvouchered funds. This practice was initiated by the OSS and has continued, with some limitations. The funds were disbursed on the Director's signature and no accounting was necessary. While this provided an unrestricted opportunity for abuse, the OSS and its successors have demonstrated a remarkable record of honesty in using unvouchered funds.

The Special Relations Office was responsible for maintaining liaison with other U.S. government organizations and with the official representatives of allied governments. It was particularly involved with the State Department, since diplomatic cover was especially useful for OSS espionage agents. OSS employees working under State Department cover were paid by State from OSS funds to further frustrate any attempts to identify their true missions.

The Technical Branches section was divided into several groups, based on the various needs of the OSS. For instance, Communications developed sophisticated radios which could be carried in suitcases and could receive as well as transmit messages. (To complete the disguise of agents using these radios, used European suitcases were purchased from pawn shops.) Research and Development worked on providing various kinds of equipment, including special weapons, authentic identification cards, and appropriate clothing.

The Research and Analysis section was divided into geographical areas. It attracted a number of university professors whose contribution to OSS and the war effort was to gain a better understanding of foreign countries and societies. Following the war, some of these people transferred to the State Department, but a number returned to academic life, where they began teaching a new branch of political science, comparative government and politics.

14

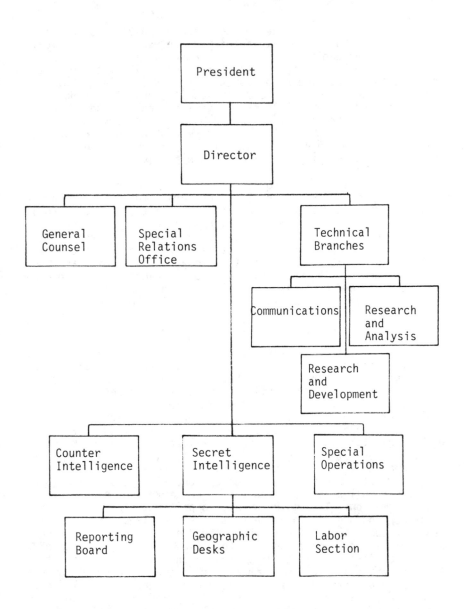

Chart 2.1 Office of Strategic Services (major elements)

15

Schools and Training served to prepare individuals for missions with the OSS. The OSS made extensive use of psychological testing and evaluation to determine the suitability of potential agents for the hazards and stresses they were likely to encounter. This was the first time such testing was used on a large scale, although it later became a commonly-accepted practice in both government and business. Another aspect of Schools and Training was The Farm, a training base in the Maryland countryside. Later transferred to Camp Peary, Virginia, by the CIA, The Farm provided advanced training in various intelligence work, from code enciphering and deciphering to weapons and explosives use.

The Special Relations Office, Technical Branches, Research and Analysis, and Schools and Training were situated in Washington. They provided the necessary support for the more glamorous and intriguing parts of the OSS which were engaged in covert operations. The roles played by these support structures were vital and perhaps more significant than those performed by the covert action side of OSS. The drama of espionage and paramilitary operations is undeniable, but the daily, routine activities of groups like Research and Analysis and Communications probably contributed more to the comprehensive war effort. Still, the covert operations represented a major part of the OSS functions and their impact on contemporary intelligence work has been profound.

The main task of Secret Intelligence (SI) was the covert collection of information not otherwise available. Information that was manifest could be easily gathered through overt means such as reading newspapers, viewing films, and debriefing refugees. Other vital information required clandestine methods. By using stealth and deception the collector not only improves his or her chances of obtaining the information but also guarantees the information will remain valid. If the "target" realizes that secret plans are known to the enemy, the plans can be changed, rendering their secrecy meaningless. Thus, to protect both the agent and the information, SI stressed the importance of concealing the sources, the methods of collection, and the techniques involved in acquiring the information. This is known as "compartmentation," and it is a basic principle of espionage that those involved in the intelligence process will know only what they "need to know." A second principle in the collection of information is the importance of nonstandardization. It is vital that agents avoid routine patterns that are suspicious, although it is equally crucial to maintain those patterns consistent with one's cover. This balance between nonstandardization in the collection and transmission of information and maintaining a plausible cover is a test of the art of espionage. The penalty for failing to properly balance these two aspects of espionage is often exposure as a spy.

A second activity of SI was conducted by its Reporting Board, which graded and evaluated agent reports. This was the beginning of the transformation of information into intelligence, and it served to determine the accuracy and reliability of incoming information. In addition to preparing the information for further processing, the Reporting Board attempted to determine when agent reports had been sent under duress (e.g., by captured agents transmitting information under the control of their captors) and when reports were being sent by double agents. Double agents are those who appear to be loyal to one side but are actually loyal to the other.

Secret Intelligence was responsible for planning the insertion of agents into enemy territory where they would appear to be legitimate, but would actually be collecting information covertly and sending that information back to the OSS.[15] Most of the postwar espionage stories focused on occupied France, but SI operated around the world. It was partially divided into Geographic Desks covering Europe, the Middle East, and the Far East. The rest of SI was functionally focused and included the Labor Section which managed to infiltrate the first OSS agent into Nazi Germany.

Counter-Espionage focused on enemy intelligence efforts. It sought to protect U.S. secrets from becoming known by the enemy, and it also attempted to penetrate the enemy's intelligence services and thereby control and manipulate the enemy's intelligence products and operations. Its initial and persistent needs included a vast body of records, most of them dealing with enemy intelligence agents and organizations, and personnel skilled in the arcane art and science of counterespionage. OSS had neither of these two basic requirements at the outset, and autonomous development of them would have taken decades of expensive (in money and lives) trial and error. Fortunately, British intelligence offered its invaluable assistance. The importance of the British contribution cannot be overemphasized.[16] As a result of its phenomenal trust, OSS had access to files and records developed by Britain's intelligence service over the years. The U.S.-British wartime union in counterespionage efforts resulted in two factors crucial to the postwar development of the American intelligence community. First, it resulted in a sizable personnel pool of highly-trained and experienced people with unique talents. While the presence of OSS counterespionage graduates did not require the creation of an organization to utilize their skills, their availability made such an organization feasible. Indeed, without such a group, a peacetime intelligence service would have been unthinkable, since counterespionage is a requisite function of any intelligence apparatus.

The second major result of the U.S.-British counterespionage collaboration was the set of personal and professional relationships that contributed to postwar exchanges of espionage material between the allied intelligence services. Some bureaucratic rivalry existed during and after the war, with Britons skeptical of the ability of OSS to protect vital secrets and Americans accusing the British of using the OSS to maintain the sagging British Empire. But the general sense of cooperation that developed during the war continued to be manifested by an allied effort after the war. Again, this relationship argued persuasively for the continuation of an espionage capability after 1945.

One other component of OSS is of particular importance. Special Operations was responsible for physical subversion of the enemy. Its activities included sabotage and support for various resistance groups. These operations were under the control and direction of military commanders, used military personnel (the physically fit were subject to the draft), and involved the OSS in "active" paramilitary activities rather than the "passive" work of collecting information and processing it into intelligence. Thus, a precedent was established of combining intelligence activities that were focused on policy planning and on policy implementation. Although the two functions are conceptually distinct, a degree of overlap inevitably occurs. In order for Research and Analysis to be aware of all of the potential ramifications of its advice to the policy makers, it had to know the potential of Special Operations. Likewise, Special Operations had to have direct and continuous communications with Research and Analysis in order to conduct its missions. So, there was a substantial bureaucratic logic about having the two seemingly disparate functions performed by a single institutional entity. This practice has been continued, despite criticisms. It is an example of bureaucratic inertia, which may or may not be beneficial or pragmatic.

The wartime performance of OSS was characterized by both successes and failures. Its direct military contributions were generally useful where local theater commanders made use of its various capabilities. It was of particular importance in the Torch invasion of North Africa and the Overlord invasion at Normandy. In both cases it produced useful and at times vital intelligence on the natural environment and social conditions at the point of attack. In contrast, its value to Douglas MacArthur's campaigns in the Southwest Pacific was marginal at best, since MacArthur preferred to rely on his own Army Intelligence and his own considerable knowledge of the area.

One area of OSS Special Operations that had considerable postwar importance was Southeast Asia. A strong, positive relationship developed between OSS officers and Ho Chi Minh in the Indochinese area.[17] This mutual personal and professional respect would result in one of the great ironies of the Vietnam War, when CIA analysts were suggesting that the U.S. could not defeat Ho's forces in a military conflict. Indeed, the CIA argued that the U.S. should reach a tacit agreement with Ho, perhaps even in the form of some sort of alliance. At the same time, other parts of the CIA were conducting vigorous paramilitary operations against Ho's forces.

The OSS also conducted intelligence and espionage operations in neutral countries. In the so-called "secondary" neutral nations of Ireland, Spain, and Portugal, these operations were primarily focused on data gathering. For instance, the Vatican representatives to Ireland greatly abused their diplomatic privileges by passing information to the OSS regarding Japanese bombing targets. Spain and Portugal were acknowledged by both sides as important spying centers and were characterized by high concentrations of counterespionage agents of various loyalties.

In the "principal" neutral countries of Sweden and Switzerland, the OSS activity was pronounced. From Sweden, OSS, together with British intelligence, provided aid and advice to the Danish and Norwegian resistance movements. However, it was Switzerland that represented our prime intelligence outpost.[18] The director of OSS activities in Switzerland was Allen Dulles, who would spend a lifetime in the intelligence business and would serve as the head of the U.S. intelligence community during its most glamorous period. Dulles managed the Swiss OSS station, which maintained a highly-productive allied "listening post," originated and maintained contact with the German anti-Hitler underground, developed relations with dissident enemy diplomats, infiltrated the German government (including its Foreign Office and its military intelligence service), acquired great amounts of military, political, and industrial intelligence (including the development of Germany's atomic bomb capabilities), and finally orchestrated the surrender of German military forces in Italy.[19] All of these activities contributed to Dulles' stature as America's foremost "spymaster" and legitimized his role in the development of the U.S. postwar intelligence service.

The progress of OSS from its incipient creation on June 11, 1941, to its demobilization on October 1, 1945, was rapid and profound. It grew into an established, bureaucratic structure performing a variety of activities crucial to the U.S. war needs. It established both domestic and international relations with potential sources of support, especially Congress at home and the British abroad. It developed a workforce with unique skills and experience. It resulted in the acceptance of covert activities and the realization of the necessity of abnormal diplomatic and political actions in a hostile environment.

The war ended and OSS was disbanded. But there was a consensual recognition that the new global role to be played by the United States demanded some form of continued intelligence organization. For nearly two years the debate over the form and control of intelligence would help characterize America's adjustment to superpower status. Some OSS sections were absorbed by the Departments of War and Navy, while others became part of the State Department. Many OSS veterans left government service, some because they felt attached to the uniqueness that had been OSS and did not want to become part of a more traditional branch of government.

The debate between the military and civilian departments over the control and operation of intelligence was finally resolved by the National Security Act of 1947, which permitted each to retain an intelligence capability germane to its primary functions, but also created the first full-fledged peacetime intelligence service in America's history, the Central Intelligence Agency. In subsequent years, the CIA was joined by other intelligence organizations to form what is now known as the intelligence community.

NOTES

1. U.S., Congress, Senate, Select Committee to Study Government Operations with Respect to Intelligence Activities, Final Report. Book VI. Supplementary Detailed Staff Reports on Foreign and Military Intelligence (Washington: Government Printing Office, 1976), Tyrus G. Fain, Katherine C. Plant, and Ross Millroy, The Intelligence Community: History, Organization, and Issues (New York: R. R. Bowker Company, 1977), Anne Karalekas, History of the Central Intelligence Agency (Laguna Hills, CA: Aegean Park Press, 1977), and William R. Corson, The Armies of Ignorance: The Rise of the American Intelligence Empire (New York: The Dial Press, 1977).

2. For an application of this argument to US-USSR relations since 1945, see Harry Howe Ransom, "Strategic Intelligence and 'Intermestic' Politics," paper delivered at the September, 1982 American Political Science Convention.

3. John Bakeless, Turncoats, Traitors, and Heros (Philadelphia: J. B. Lippincott Company, 1959).

4. Vincent and Nan Buranelli, Spy/Counterspy: An Encyclopedia of Espionage (New York: McGraw-Hill Book Company, 1982), pp. 9-10.

5. Ibid., p. 144.

6. Richard Wilmer Rowan, The Story of Secret Service (Garden City, NY: Doubleday, Doran and Company, Inc., 1937).

7. John Bakeless, Spies of the Confederacy (Philadelphia: J. B. Lippincott Company, 1970). Civil War History, 10 (December 1964).

8. Herbert O. Yardley, The American Black Chamber (Indianapolis: Bobbs-Merrill, 1931).

9. William Stevenson, A Man Called Intrepid (New York: Ballantine Books, 1976), Corey Ford, Donovan of OSS (Boston: Little, Brown and Company, 1970), and Thomas F. Troy, Donovan and the CIA: A History of the Establishment of the Central Intelligence Agency (Washington: Central Intelligence Agency, 1981).

10. War Report of the OSS (Office of Strategic Services), 2 vols. (New York: Walker and Company, 1976) and R. Harris Smith, OSS: The Secret History of America's First Central Intelligence Agency (Berkeley: University of California Press, 1972), Chapter One.

11. Roberta Wholstetter, Pearl Harbor: Warning and Decision (Stanford: Stanford University Press, 1962) and "Cuba and Pearl Harbor," Foreign Affairs, 43 (July 1965) and Ladislas Farago, The Broken Seal: The Story of "Operation MAGIC" and the Pearl Harbor Disaster (New York: Random House, 1967).

12. War Report of the OSS and Troy, op. cit.

13. Smith, op. cit.

14. Ibid., War Report of the OSS, William Colby, Honorable Men: My Life in the CIA (New York: Simon and Schuster, 1978), and Thomas Powers, The Man Who Kept the Secrets: Richard Helms and the CIA (New York: Alfred A. Knopf, 1979).

15. Joseph E. Perisco, Piercing the Reich: The Penetration of Nazi Germany by American Secret Agents during World War II (New York: Viking Press, 1979).

16. Stevenson, op. cit.

17. Harris, op. cit., Chapter 10 and Archimedes L. A. Patti, Why Viet Nam? Prelude to America's Albatross (Berkeley: University of California Press, 1980).

18. Leonard Mosely, Dulles: A Biography of Eleanor, Allen and John Foster Dulles and Their Family Network (New York: The Dial Press, 1978).

19. Allen W. Dulles, The Secret Surrender (New York: Harper and Row, 1966).

CHAPTER 3

The Intelligence Community[1]

Introduction

It has been suggested that the term "intelligence community" is a misnomer. "Community" implies a sense of unification, especially regarding compatible association to work together toward some common goal or set of goals. If this is how we choose to interpret the term, the intelligence apparatus of the United States government is a community in the technical sense that it is a collection of elements sharing a common purpose -- to produce intelligence useful for the purposes of policy planning. However, the elements that constitute the intelligence community are fragmented by bureaucratic divisions that often preclude a unified effort at producing intelligence. At times, the community has been characterized by disunity and severe disagreement over basic intelligence "facts" as well as conclusions. So, the collection of organizations, bureaus, agencies, and departments that are commonly known as the intelligence community often does not act in a communal fashion. Nonetheless, the term has been used so pervasively that it has become part of the popular lexicon, and is a useful term despite its conceptual and semantical weaknesses.[2]

There are several fundamental characteristics about the intelligence community.[3] Perhaps the most important of these is that its membership is subject to frequent and rapid change. Because the operative components are in the executive branch of government, it is the President and his advisors who decide which elements will constitute the intelligence machinery. Every president has restructured the community in some fashion since its inception in 1947. Frequently the restructuring occurs early in an Administration, but minor changes may continue throughout any one president's tenure. This constant flux means that any attempt to fully describe the structures of the intelligence community is doomed to rapid obsolescence.

A second basic feature of the intelligence community permits a useful answer to this dilemma. While the community is always undergoing some actual or planned change, certain key elements are always present and of major importance. These structures represent the core of the intelligence community. By virtue of the kind of intelligence they process, the bureaucratic strength they represent, and in general their institutionalized roles as intelligence community members, these organizations represent the focal point of any analyses and observations about U.S. national strategic intelligence. From a structural viewpoint, the community is composed of constants and variables. The constants are the main institutions and the variables are the peripheral bureaus that

23

are added or subtracted, based primarily on the perspectives and goals of the President and his key advisors. Among these advisors, the one who normally has the major responsibility for organizing the intelligence community is the Special Assistant to the President for National Security. He is the titular head of the National Security Council, which, as Chart 3.1 shows, is the key link between the community and the President.

Community Components

National Security Council (NSC).[4] The National Security Council was established by the National Security Act of 1947, which also reorganized the U.S. military and created the CIA. The NSC is part of the Executive Office of the President, and consequently is intended to be responsive to the President. As a presidential tool, its use is determined primarily by the occupant of the Oval Office. Since 1947, different presidents have used the NSC in a variety of ways. The basic function of the NSC is to assist the President in planning, integrating, and implementing the nation's security policy. Specifically, the NSC examines and determines national security threats and goals, attempts to coordinate policies that transcend bureaucratic divisions (e.g., policies that involve the State Department, the Pentagon, and elements of the intelligence community), and advises the President on possible policy options. The NSC is the primary link between the President and the intelligence community.

As a policy planning unit, the NSC necessarily must have reliable, accurate, and timely intelligence. Because the majority of national security policy is directed at foreign nations (both allies and adversaries), the NSC relies to a great extent on the intelligence community for input. The Special Assistant for National Security heads a staff of analysts, but the NSC depends on the vast intelligence apparatus for the data that is a prerequisite for analysis. The relationship between the NSC and the intelligence community is a symbiotic one in which the two interact continually. The NSC issues requests for intelligence on specific national security porblems and uses the resultant intelligence to produce NSC outputs. Simultaneously, the intelligence community produces intelligence as a result of its own activities and some of this intelligence is brought to the attention of the NSC.

This conceptually harmonious relationship often works well, but sometimes fails to operate effectively. Many factors cause the system to malfunction. Chief among these dysfunctional factors (covered more extensively in Chapter 5) are the disunity of the intelligence community, which is manifested in conflicting and sometimes even contradictory intelligence reports flowing to the NSC, and lack of confidence in the skill and/or responsiveness of one party by the other.[5] The national security machinery

24

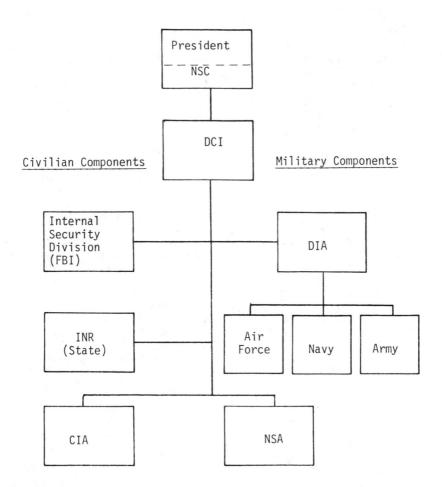

Chart 3.1 The U.S. Intelligence Community

has the potential to coordinate the various elements of the system in a cohesive and rational way, but that coordination rarely is completely satisfactory and sometimes contributes to "intelligence failures" and poor planning by its absence.[6] Another factor that hinders the smooth operation of the machinery is the changes in the way the NSC is used by the President.[7] While the intelligence community is fairly stable over a period of time, the NSC experiences more frequent personnel turnovers. It also reflects the different attitudes, perceptions, and other personal attributes of different presidents.

Central Intelligence Agency (CIA). To many people, the CIA is synonymous with the intelligence community. The fallacy of this misconception is illustrated by the facts that it is neither the largest nor the most expensive component of the intelligence community, as Table 3.1 illustrates. Its importance and visibility stem from its assigned role as the coordinating and directing unit of the U.S. intelligence community, as well as its actual role as the principal espionage and covert action actor in the U.S. government. It continues to be the major structure in the intelligence community and it rightly deserves a separate chapter.

Defense Intelligence Agency (DIA).[9] The DIA was created in 1961, in part as the response to the ill-conceived, misguided, and poorly-executed Bay of Pigs invasion. At the urging of the Director of Central Intelligence (Allen Dulles) and the Joint Chiefs of Staff, President Kennedy endorsed a U.S.-sponsored attempt to land a military force of Cuban expatriates with the intent of inspiring a popular uprising to depose the Castro regime. Dulles overruled his own CIA analysts and predicted the Cuban people would join the invaders to overthrow the Castro regime. Kennedy agreed to the invasion, despite his misgivings about the wisdom of the plan, in large part because of Dulles' persuasive arguments regarding latent anti-Castroism among the Cuban people. This invasion was a disaster, the Cuban people did not support the invaders, and Kennedy blamed the CIA.

The Bay of Pigs represents a major event in the evolution of the U.S. intelligence community. As a result of this foreign policy failure, Kennedy had little faith in the CIA as the sole supplier of intelligence. While he realized the Agency was an indispensable structure, he wanted to have alternative intelligence sources upon which to base foreign and national security policy decisions. The most reasonable alternative source of intelligence was the military. Because each of the services had its own intelligence component, it was relatively easy to create the Defense Intelligence Agency, which would coordinate and manage the disparate components of military intelligence.

Analysis of the CIA includes two basic perspectives. One

Table 3.1

Size and Cost of U.S. Intelligence Community Components[8]

Component	Personnel*	Budget*
CIA	12	15
DIA	4	4
Air Force (including NRO)	35	40
Navy	12	10
Army	20	12
NSA	16	18
INR	**	**
Internal Security (FBI)	**	**
Total	100	100

*in approximate percentages. The actual figures vary across time, depending on circumstances that effect presidential and congressional attitudes toward the intelligence community. The figures are classified, although every year legislation is introduced to declassify at least the macro figures. Thus, actual figures are subject to inevitable change. However, the percentages remain fairly constant and therefore are more useful comparative measures. For those who insist on actual figures, the totals for 1980 were approximately 200,000 personnel and a budget of nearly $10 billion.

**less than one percent.

view looks at its internal role as a coordinating and supervising unit. In the late 1950s each of the three services produced a number of intelligence analyses that concluded that a "missile gap" existed between the strategic nuclear forces of the U.S. and the USSR. Furthermore, the gap was disadvantageous for the United States since, these analyses claimed, the Russians were in the lead in nuclear arms. While there was agreement on these basic conclusions, the specific nature of the missile gap varied, with each service attempting to justify its own budgetary and functional demands. The analyses were self-serving conclusions, but the general situation seemed clear and definite, despite CIA arguments that no such gap existed or, if it did, the U.S. was far ahead of the Soviets in nuclear weapons.

The DIA was created to remedy this sort of bureaucratic debate. Its responsibilities include managing the various military intelligence activities so that coordinated and objective analyses will be produced. It has several other responsibilities, including supervision and management of Department of Defense intelligence operations, but it is the DIA contribution to the intelligence product that is the primary concern of the NSC. The extent to which the DIA successfully performs this role is open to debate. In some cases coordination is virtually impossible since the DIA is attempting to coordinate and direct autonomous and bureaucratically strong units. The individual services continue to compete with each other for budget appropriations and task assignments. In other cases, the DIA is relatively successful in presenting unified analyses supported by all of the services. This was especially evident during the Vietnam War, when the Pentagon challenged the CIA for the right to define the nature of the struggle.[10] This subject is dealt with in more detail in Chapter 5, but the basic dispute centered on whether the war was a political and social struggle, as the CIA argued, or whether it was a military problem, which the Pentagon contended. The ability of the DIA to unify the military intelligence analyses and estimates was crucial to the ultimate success of the Pentagon in this case.

The second basic analytical perspective of the DIA focuses on its external relations. The case of the CIA-DIA debate over the nature of the Vietnam War illustrates that the internal-external division is somewhat artificial, but the internal-external dimensions of administrative behavior are useful in helping us understand the DIA as a bureaucratic entity. The basic external function of the Defense Intelligence Agency is to help represent the Pentagon in the intelligence community. As we have seen, this "community" has few communal affections and is frequently characterized by agency egoism that results in debate and division. The DIA is the official military representative to the community and it is entitled to know about plans and operations of other community members. As the Vietnam case shows, it also plays an integral part in producing general intelligence reports from the community to the NSC.

The DIA has a large staff and a fairly-sizable budget. Accurate contemporary figures are protected for security reasons, but a reasonable estimate is that its budget is about one-fourth the size of the CIA's and it has approximately one-third the CIA's personnel. Since the DIA does not engage in any meaningful amounts of intelligence collection or analyses, but concentrates on the administrative functions of coordination and management, its resources permit it to be competitive with the CIA. Its routine activities include supervision of the overt military attaches who are assigned to U.S. embassies around the world and who collect information in an overt manner, and the preparation of daily and weekly intelligence reports that are distributed throughout the Pentagon and the entire intelligence community. Since it serves as a clearinghouse for military intelligence it depends greatly on the intelligence components of the three services for information gathering and intelligence production. Each of these services is larger in size and budget than the DIA, which gives them bureaucratic strength that is complemented by their separate institutional bases.

Air Force Intelligence. The primary responsibility of Air Force Intelligence (S-2) is the observation and analysis of potential and actual capabilities of other nations' tactical and strategic air forces. Of special concern is the strategic nuclear posture of the Soviet Union. These tasks are of critical importance to the national security of the United States, and consequently S-2 is a high-priority intelligence community component.[11] It must maintain records of current force levels of other nations as well as their current research and development programs. It must monitor and evaluate both quantitative and qualitative changes in foreign arsenals in order to assess U.S. air defense needs accurately and reliably. Because these changes reflect the rapid progress of ever-greater technological sophistication, Air Force Intelligence has become the most expensive and largest member of the intelligence community.[12]

Air Force Intelligence represents approximately one-third of intelligence community personnel. This means it is about three times the size of the CIA. Its budget is roughly 40 percent of the total community budget and is over three times the budget of the CIA. The main reason for its disproportionate size and cost lies in the nature of the data it necessarily must collect and the methods of collection it employs. In order to accomplish its primary task, S-2 uses the more sophisticated and expensive forms of technological acquisition. Because its major concern is the nuclear capability of the Soviet Union, it must continually observe what the Soviets are doing in this field. The most reliable means of observation is the satellite or "spy in the sky."[13]

The United States maintains several satellites in stationary orbit over the Soviet Union. Operating over a hundred miles above the target, these satellites rotate with the earth so that they remain fixed over a target area, although they can be shifted to cover other areas of the globe. They are maintained and operated by the main structure of Air Force Intelligence, the National Reconnaissance Office (NRO), which uses about 60 percent of the Air Force Intelligence budget. Most of these funds pay for the placement and maintenance of the satellites. The NRO operates the data-gathering satellite programs for the entire intelligence community and is responsive to the needs of various community members. For instance, during the 1973 Yom Kippur War in the Middle East, data obtained by the NRO via its satellites detected the movement of elite Soviet troop units, together with their equipment, to staging bases in the USSR. Administration officials were able to use this information to warn the Soviet leaders that the presence of Soviet troops in support of their Middle East allies would require a similar escalation by the United States, thus transforming the war into a direct confrontation between combat units of the two superpowers. Similar cases exist that illustrate that the NRO serves the needs of the entire intelligence community. However, the routine, daily collection of satellite data directly and continually serves Air Force Intelligence.

The fundamental concern of Air Force Intelligence is the current state of the Soviet strategic nuclear forces. Because Soviet nuclear doctrine stresses the Inter-Continental Ballistic Missile (ICBM) as the primary means of delivering nuclear warheads, it is incumbent on Air Force Intelligence to know where the ICBMs are located and what their operational characteristics are. The satellites operated by the NRO utilize a variety of means to acquire these data.

One important way of obtaining information on Soviet nuclear capabilities is to take pictures. Intelligence that results from photographs is called PHOTINT, and the photography done by the NRO's satellites reflects the latest in technology. From a height of over 100 miles, these cameras can penetrate cloud cover and also photograph at night. Their high-resolution lenses are so advanced that they can identify individual vehicles by their license plate numbers. PHOTINT is a vital means of knowing what types of weapons systems are being deployed in what locations. When analyzed and integrated with other data, PHOTINT enables Air Force Intelligence to predict Soviet strategic intentions. Photographs from space are a major benefit of satellite surveillance, but it is not the only type of data acquired by the NRO.

In addition to PHOTINT, NRO satellites and other equipment are sensitive to electronic impulses (ELINT), signals emitted from various targets (SIGINT), and communications (COMINT).[14] All of these means of data acquisition produce information of value to various intelligence community structures, but again, it is Air Force Intelligence that is a direct and regular beneficiary. Whenever the Soviet Union tests a missile, the preliminary indications are unmistakable, and in some cases are even openly announced in order to prevent any misunderstanding by the United States. The "spy in the sky" uses its technology to monitor the test and, when these data are analyzed, Air Force Intelligence has greater knowledge of Soviet capabilities in terms of factors such as payload, number and types of warheads, speed, accuracy, and range.

While knowledge of Soviet nuclear capability remains the primary goal of Air Force Intelligence, it has a wide range of interests relating to air forces throughout the world. It maintains data files on the number, types, and status of the air force capabilities of virtually every nation. These files are updated from a variety of intelligence sources, including other community members and the U.S. Air Force attaches assigned to U.S. embassies throughout the world. These attaches supply the major portion of human intelligence (HUMINT) that is input to the Air Force Intelligence process, but it is important to realize that such input represents a small percentage of the total when compared to the technical sources.[15]

Naval Intelligence. This, along with Army Intelligence, is the oldest intelligence organization in the community.[16] From the time of the American Revolution until the development of a credible offensive capability by the Soviet Union in the 1960s, the greatest potential military threat to the United States was a naval one. Although the U.S. pursued a policy of isolation from Great Power politics throughout the 19th century, the need for vigilance remained. Since Canada and Mexico represented minor threats at best, the seas to the east and west provided the only realistic avenues of attack. Also, America has always been a maritime nation which emphasizes access to overseas economic markets. Thus, U.S. military intelligence has always emphasized knowledge of foreign navies. This emphasis continues today and maintenance of America's lines of communication (LOC) and sea transport remains a paramount national security concern. Consequently, naval intelligence is a vital part of the U.S. intelligence community.

The Office of Naval Intelligence (ONI) is approximately the same size as the CIA and has a budget that represents nearly one-tenth of the entire intelligence community funds. Unlike Air Force Intelligence, which always is assured of a large appropriation due to its National Reconnaissance Office, ONI's budget and manpower allocations vary with the importance of specific naval programs. However, like the Air Force, the Navy must maintain accurate records on the various other navies of the world and thus is always guaranteed a secure base within the intelligence community. Most of the work of ONI is routine updating of information relating to naval capabilities of allies and adversaries.

An important adjunct to carrying out this task is the use of naval vessels to acquire information. Two cases of such use were revealed in the 1960s. In August of 1964, two U.S. destroyers were assisting South Vietnamese military personnel who were conducting a series of raids into North Vietnam. Among other activities, these U.S. naval vessels were using sophisticated electronic and radar devices to locate North Vietnamese defense stations and to interfere with other North Vietnamese defense measures.[17] The North Vietnamese attacked the two U.S. ships in the Tonkin Gulf, an event that precipitated U.S. escalation in that war. While the Tonkin Gulf incident and its relevance to the Vietnam War are not our concern here, it is important to note that the destroyers Maddox and Turner Joy were engaged in intelligence activities at the time.

Another notable example of the use of the Navy for intelligence gathering involved the USS Pueblo.[18] Unlike the Tonkin Gulf destroyers, the Pueblo was primarily a "spy ship." It was designed specifically to collect data rather than engage in offensive engagements. Its mission was exclusively to collect ELINT, SIGINT, and COMINT. It used advanced technology to "stimulate" the coastal and inland radar sites of North Korea and to record the responses to those stimuli. This information enabled the analysts to know what types of radar the North Koreans had, what kinds of capabilities the radars possessed, and how to counteract those radars should it become necessary. Another activity performed by the Pueblo was to listen to and record communications in and over North Korea. Specifically, voice communications between North Korean pilots were useful in determining levels of morale, unit designations and locations, aircraft performance characteristics, and individual personnel profiles. It is important to note that the operation of the sophisticated intelligence-gathering equipment was conducted by and for the National Security Agency (NSA), not ONI. However, ONI provided the Pueblo as a platform for the equipment and directly profited from the information collected. The North Koreans became aware of the mission of the Pueblo, seized it with little effort, incarcerated its crew for over a year on charges of espionage, and benefited greatly from the inability of the intelligence personnel to destroy much of the sophisticated equipment on board.

32

These examples indicate that the Navy uses modern means to acquire its intelligence. Like the Air Force, it has an extensive network of attaches around the world, but it relies primarily on technology to fulfill its basic intelligence task which is to be the chief supplier of naval intelligence for the community.

Army Intelligence.[19] Army Intelligence is the least mechanized of the three service members of the community. This is understandable, since both the Air Force and Navy rely on more complicated and sophisticated equipment and because the acquisition of information by the Air Force and Navy requires the use of satellites and ships. Another reason is that the basic mission of Army Intelligence is to collect and analyze tactical intelligence to support its forces in the event of a land war. But despite its less technological orientation the annual budget of Army Intelligence is nearly equal to that of the CIA, or slightly more than 10 percent of the total intelligence community budget. And, Army Intelligence is more than twice the size of the CIA in manpower, with more than 20 percent of the total intelligence community personnel.

The reason for this apparent paradox lies in the type of information Army Intelligence collects, analyzes, and disseminates. Its primary concern is the war potential of other nations. Since changes in troop strengths, commanding officers and generals, training and readiness levels, weapons, and tactical capabilities are far more frequent in the Army of any nation than in its Navy or Air Force, more intelligence personnel are required to monitor and audit those changes.

A second reason for what seems to be the relatively high cost and large size of Army Intelligence is the necessity of keeping maps updated. In order for the Army to be ready to respond appropriately to threats to the vital interests of the United States, Army Intelligence is concerned with cartography on a world-wide scale. Changes in topography are of great importance in anticipating combat needs, and maintaining reliable military maps is an expensive task.

Within days of the seizure of the U.S. embassy in Teheran, Iran, U.S. troops were training for the attempt to rescue the hostages. While the training continued for nearly five months before the mission was approved by the President and the National Security Council, without adequate maps the mission would have been delayed even further. Army Intelligence was able to supply the necessary maps so that the planning could begin almost immediately. Without this vital ingredient, the Army would be unable to perform its mission under any circumstances.

Army Intelligence is even more dependent on its attache system

33

than the Navy or the Air Force. The Army has more attaches in
more countries than either of its sister services, and these
attaches provide more useful information, since the Army is less
concerned with the kinds of information acquired through technological means. So, HUMINT is far more important to the Army,
although it is important to note that collection of information
by Army attaches does not necessarily imply covert or clandestine
activities. Often, the information is routinely acquired in the
course of open exchanges between U.S. and foreign attaches. Indeed, this is frequently part of the agreement whereby attaches
are sent abroad.

While HUMINT is more common to Army Intelligence, information
acquired through technological means is important also. Satellite
and other PHOTINT information is a vital aspect of cartography.
COMINT and SIGINT also provide Army Intelligence with data that
is critical to maintaining accurate and reliable intelligence.
Thus, all three services combine all forms of information
acquisition to fulfill their general and specific intelligence
tasks.

It is clear that the military is a significant part of the
intelligence community. This is understandable since the basic
purpose of an intelligence service is to enhance a country's
national security. National security policy making is inextri-
cably linked to a nation's defense, and in order to maintain a
vigilant and prepared military posture, knowledge of the military
capabilities of both friends and foes is necessary. This fundamental point is the rationale for the preeminence of the military
in the intelligence community -- nearly two-thirds of its personnel and its budget. In addition, one of the main civilian components of the community has close ties to the Defense Department
and in some ways is an extension of military intelligence.

National Security Agency.[20] The National Security Agency (NSA)
is the most secret and secretive of the major units of the intelligence community. It was created in 1952 by President Truman,
but its charter remains highly classified. Despite this emphasis
on secrecy, certain characteristics of the NSA have become public
knowledge.

NSA is a semi-autonomous agency. It is formally a part of
the Department of Defense, as is DIA and the intelligence components of the three armed services. This formal relationship
has one distinct advantage since the NSA budget and some of its
activities can be concealed as military rather than intelligence
matters. However, despite this formal connection with the
Defense Department, NSA has jurisdictional and structural
sovereignty. It is a separate member of the intelligence community and is not directed by the Joint Chiefs of Staff. Also,

its sovereignty means it is not part of the interservice rivalry that characterizes Pentagon politics. So, even though NSA is always directed by a general or admiral, NSA is in a position to serve the entire intelligence community fairly and objectively.

The National Security Agency is a large and expensive part of the intelligence community. Its budget is between 15 and 20 percent of the total intelligence community budget, about equal to that of the National Reconnaissance Office, and it employs about 15 percent of all intelligence community personnel. It is housed in a $50 million complex of buildings at Fort Meade, Maryland, which is the largest government installation in the Washington, D.C. area. (Its nearly 2,000,000 square feet of space compares to CIA headquarters floor space of 1,135,000 square feet.) An interesting feature of its Operations Building is the longest unobstructed corridor in the United States, 980 feet. Like CIA headquarters, NSA's facilities provide all the modern conveniences, including barber shops, gift shops, medical facilities, and cafeterias. The reasons for the intense secrecy and relatively high cost of the NSA lie in the main function it performs for the U.S. intelligence community.

The primary purpose of the NSA is to serve as the chief communicator for U.S. intelligence. It operates over a thousand "interception stations" around the world which rely heavily on machines and technology to record and transmit a variety of types of communications, including ELINT, SIGINT, and COMINT. In order to understand the significance of the NSA, it is necessary to appreciate the critical importance of communications to the intelligence process.

The processing of information into intelligence useful for the purposes of planning depends on the timely, reliable, accurate and secure transmission of that information to those who evaluate and analyze it and integrate it with other data to produce and distribute intelligence to policy makers. If the information is not transmitted as quickly as possible, events may occur before adequate plans can be made. If the information is not transmitted in a reliable way, evaluators and analysts may discount the information even though it may be valid and crucial to the intelligence product. If the information is inaccurate, the resulting intelligence product may lead to inappropriate plans and policies. And if the transmission is insecure, others may be able to formulate plans to jeopardize or otherwise effectively deal with any plans based on the information. Thus, effective communications is perhaps the single most important aspect of intelligence, and the NSA exists to provide this service for the U.S. intelligence community.

A primary task of the NSA is cryptography, the science of communications. The NSA is entrusted with protecting the security of messages sent between U.S. diplomatic and military installations. Using the most advanced computers and emphasizing language and mathematics skills, NSA personnel are engaged in a continual effort to create "unbreakable" communications schemes of codes and ciphers. Simultaneously, the NSA attempts to break the codes and ciphers used by other international actors so that U.S. intelligence may be able to intercept messages and know what those communications mean.

The ELINT, SIGINT, and COMINT are collected by NSA machines at its interception stations. These may be on satellites operated by the National Reconnaissance Office of Air Force Intelligence, on naval vessels such as the Pueblo operated by Naval Intelligence, at ground installations operated by Army Intelligence, in embassies, consulates, or other diplomatic and economic offices of the U.S. government located abroad, or at installations operated exclusively by NSA. Much of the NSA data-collection effort is targeted at the USSR, and the periphery of the Soviet Union is ringed by NSA operations. Through the use of sophisticated equipment, the NSA collects enormous amounts of information which must then be processed to separate the trivial from the important. Several examples will indicate the utility of NSA information to national-security planning.

The Soviet strategic rocket test range lies on a west-to-east axis that begins near the Iranian border and ends in Siberia. Before the Iranian revolution, NSA maintained two interception stations in northern Iran that were situated so that the collection devices, emphasizing SIGINT, could track the Soviet missiles. This enabled the U.S. to monitor the accuracy, speed, size, and other vital characteristics of the Soviet missiles. The missiles sent telemetry data to ground stations and these signals were received by the two NSA stations in Iran. It should be noted that the signals were in code, which meant the code had to be broken, but the intelligence process began with the collection of data. The loss of these two sites as a result of the Iranian revolution has impaired U.S. intelligence capabilities in monitoring Soviet missile tests.

In another case, the NSA was able to monitor conversations between high-ranking Soviet officials as they rode through the streets of Moscow and spoke to each other on their car telephones. This operation continued for a number of years until it was discovered by the Soviets, primarily as a result of an article in the Western press. This case reveals the intense competition between the Soviets and Western intelligence, especially the NSA, in trying to listen in on privileged information and communications. The secrecy of the NSA is understandable given the vital nature of the transmission of information and intelligence.

Bureau of Intelligence and Research.[21] This intelligence community component is part of the State Department. It has existed, in one form or another, since the creation of the State Department in 1789. Knowledge of the foreign-policy intentions and activities of other nations is an obvious and traditional concern of any nation's foreign ministry. Without such knowledge, a country is unable to make its own plans and policies. Since nations do not exist or operate in a vacuum, intelligence about other international actors is a basic part of any foreign policy.

This rationale has not resulted in a consistent appreciation of the necessity for an intelligence-producing capability in the State Department. During the 19th century, when America pursued a foreign policy that combined commercial involvement in the world simultaneously with international political isolation or noninvolvement, the State Department intelligence process was haphazard and unsystematic. The process emphasized opportunities for business success, although it included political concerns when potential crises arose. Since these crises were infrequent, due in large part to our general isolationist policy, there was no concerted effort to bring order or management to foreign policy intelligence. Indeed, we were attempting, with some success, to operate in a political vacuum. When a crisis arose, the War and Navy Departments became the main organs of intelligence production.

This attitude of benign neglect of political intelligence continued into the 20th century. It was perhaps best expressed by Henry Stimson who, when he became Secretary of State in 1928 and learned of a State Department unit that was trying to break the secret diplomatic codes of other nations, abolished the unit with the argument that "Gentlemen do not read each other's mail." While this perception of international politics is extremely naive in today's international setting, it does reflect the view of diplomats and the State Department in the period before World War II, the beginning of the Cold War era, and the organization and establishment of the U.S. intelligence community. Intelligence is now regarded as a vital and legitimate concern of the State Department, and the Bureau of Intelligence and Research (INR) is a constant, albeit minor, part of the intelligence community.

The budget and size of INR is miniscule compared to the CIA, NSA, and military elements of the intelligence community. Its budget rarely exceeds $10 million or about .1 percent of the total intelligence budget. Its personnel number in the low hundreds, compared to the tens of thousands of Army and Air Force

37

Intelligence. It has no formal collection capability of its own
and depends on State Department diplomatic cables and memoranda
and on the periodic reports from the rest of the intelligence
community for its data. Its main function is to analyze diplomatic activities of other nations and to represent the State
Department on various intelligence community panels and boards.
As a result of the rivalry between the State Department and the
National Security Council in making and executing foreign policy,
INR remains a minor participant.

Internal Security Division.[22] This is a branch of the Federal
Bureau of Investigation (FBI) which has primary responsibility for
counterespionage, defined as the defense of the United States
against penetration by the intelligence services of other nations.
The FBI, of course, has a number of law enforcement functions,
but Internal Security represents its linkage to the intelligence
community. Because its parent organization is primarily concerned
with domestic rather than foreign affairs, Internal Security has
developed what amounts to an inferiority complex. While its
intelligence community function is vital to the national security
and to the rest of the intelligence community, it does not have
a foreign focus in its operations.

The jurisdiction of Internal Security reflects this dilemma.
The identification, observation, and manipulation and/or exposure
of foreign agents working in the U.S. cannot be neatly defined by
geographical boundaries. Since the CIA is statutorily restricted
from domestic counterespionage activities and the FBI has only
limited foreign operations, cooperation is crucial to any organized counterespionage capability. Information about potential
or actual foreign agents and operations must be exchanged between the FBI and the other members of the intelligence community.
However, the necessary exchange mechanisms have never been
instituted and have even been deliberately ignored at times.

This was especially true toward the end of the J. Edgar
Hoover era of the FBI. Hoover had virtually created the FBI and
directed its growth to prominence as an incorruptible organ for
law enforcement and counterespionage. He jealously defended its
bureaucratic boundaries and developed a fundamental sense of
conflict with any other agencies that attempted to usurp the
established FBI functions. He successfully denied the OSS jurisdiction over Latin America during World War II, arguing that it
was an area best covered by the FBI. He resisted post-war
intrusions by the foreign-oriented intelligence community components into domestic operations. His defense of bureaucratic
functional boundaries became most obvious when, in the late
1960s, he forbade FBI agents from having any contact with CIA
personnel without his authorization. This reduced the effectiveness of America's counterespionage efforts at a time when the

Administration was acutely concerned that the more radical and violent elements in U.S. society were being aided and abetted from abroad. Despite Hoover's edicts, information was transmitted between FBI personnel and others in the intelligence community, but the flow of this information was greatly impaired.

Subsequent Directors of the FBI have made changes in the Bureau's relationships with the rest of the intelligence community and have tried to improve the flow of counterespionage information and the entire counterespionage process. However, the relationship of Internal Security to the rest of the community remains a tenuous one, for several reasons. The FBI operates almost exclusively in the domestic arena while the CIA, NSA, INR, and military intelligence units are primarily concerned with events abroad. Internal Security is a minor component of the FBI while the other community members are major components of their various parent agencies and departments. The personal and bureaucratic relationships of the Hoover era continue to be manifested, especially as the mid-level bureaucrats of that era move into high-level positions in their respective organizations. Finally, Internal Security has neither the manpower (less than 1,000) nor the budget (approximately 10 percent of CIA's) to be anything but a minor part of the community, despite its critical function.

Others. The structures discussed above are the central and constant members of the intelligence community. Other participants are added and/or subtracted, depending on the way new Administrations prefer to organize the intelligence community. A list of all of the peripheral and often transitory members is useful only if it is understood that they are not always part of the community and that they are only infrequently critical to the intelligence process or product. These minor members often include representatives from the Treasury Department, the Drug Enforcement Agency or its equivalent, the Department of Energy (especially that part concerned with nuclear energy), and various ad hoc committees designed to review the performance of the intelligence community and its main component. One of these committees is of special importance. It has been called the 303 Committee, the Forty Committee, the Operations Advisory Committee, the Special Action Group, and other important-sounding but semantically meaningless titles.

This unit is a group of foreign policy elites who may or may not have official governmental positions. Membership in the group is determined by the President, although it almost always includes the Secetaries of State and Defense, the President's National Security Advisor, the Director of Central Intelligence, the Chairman of the Joint Chiefs of Staff, and the Director of the Office of Management and Budget. Other participants include personal and/or political advisors and confidantes of the President. The purpose of this group is to review especially sensitive covert operations proposed by or conducted by the intelligence community and to advise the President on their potential benefits and costs. It is independent from the formal intelligence community apparatus and theoretically it serves as a monitoring and auditing agency for covert operations.

This unit has several goals. One is to enhance the foreign policy and national security of the United States by correlating specific covert operations with the general policy of America. A second objective is to assess the utility of such operations compared to more open, direct activities. Another concern of this group is to avoid embarrassment for the President and the U.S. should the operation be uncovered as the work of U.S. intelligence. The group is not funded and has no official status. It may meet regularly but often it adopts a more informal approach to its work. It should be emphasized that this collection of elites is only concerned with the most sensitive operations of U.S. intelligence, and its relative importance and relevance are largely determined by the President's perception of the propriety and utility of such operations.

Conclusion

The intelligence community is composed of varied elements from throughout the executive branch. While both the Senate and House of Representatives have standing committees on intelligence, the community is effectively an exclusively Executive Branch phenomenon. It is dominated by military units. Its concerns focus on foreign policy and national security. It appears to be structurally cohesive but it has so many potentially conflictful members that centralizing and coordinating the intelligence process are difficult, if not impossible, tasks. Thus, it is a structural community that is more confederal than unified. However, there is one part of the community that is responsible for unifying and coordinating the intelligence process and product, the Central Intelligence Agency. This chapter has shown that the CIA is not the largest, not the most expensive, and in some cases not the most important processor in the community. However, it is the most visible community member and it remains the focal point of U.S. intelligence.

NOTES

1. U. S., Congress, House, Select Committee on Intelligence,
   Hearings (Washington: Government Printing Office, 1976) and
   U. S., Congress, Senate, Select Committee to Study Governmental Operations with Respect to Intelligence Activities,
   Hearings and Final Report (Washington: Government Printing
   Office, 1976). In 1975 these two committees, known respec-
   tively as the Pike Committee and the Church Committee,
   reviewed the components, activities, and issues of the intel-
   ligence community. Of particular relevance to this Chapter
   are Parts I and II of the Pike Committee Hearings and Books I,
   IV, and VI of the Church Committee Hearings. Also see U. S.
   Commission on the Organization of the Government for the
   Conduct of Foreign Policy. Report (Washington: U. S. Government Printing Office, 1975) and U. S., Senate, Select Committee on Intelligence, National Intelligence Reorganization and
   Reform Act of 1978, Hearings (Washington: Government Printing
   Office, 1978).

2. Harry Howe Ransom, The Intelligence Establishment (Cambridge,
   MA: Harvard University Press, 1970) and Lyman B. Kirkpatrick,
   Jr., The U. S. Intelligence Community: Foreign and Domestic
   Activities (New York: Hill and Wang, 1973).

3. Keith C. Clark and Lawrence J. Legere, eds., The President and
   the Management of National Security: A Report by the Institute
   for Defense Analysis (New York: Praeger, 1969).

4. Ibid. and Amos A. Jordan, William J. Taylor, Jr., and Associ-
   ates, American National Security: Policy and Process (Baltimore: The John Hopkins University Press, 1981).

5. Edmund S. Hawley, "The Administration of the Intelligence
   Community," Monograph on National Security Affairs (Providence,
   RI: Brown University, June 1976).

6. Bruce O. Reidel, "Intelligence Failures in the October War,"
   Monograph on National Security Affairs (Providence, RI: Brown
   University, June 1976).

7. Ray S. Cline, "Policy Without Intelligence," Foreign Policy,
   17 (Winter 1974-5).

8. Victor L. Marchetti and John D. Marks, The CIA and the Cult of
   Intelligence (New York: Alfred A. Knopf, 1974) and U. S.,
   House, Select Committee on Intelligence, Hearings. Part 1.
   U. S. Intelligence Agencies and Activities: Costs and Fiscal
   Procedures (Washington: Government Printing Office, 1976).

41

9. U. S., Senate, Select Committee to Study Governmental Operations with Respect to Intelligence Activities, Final Report.
   Book I. Foreign and Military Intelligence and Final Report.
   Book VI. Supplementary Detailed Staff Reports on Foreign and
   Military Intelligence (Washington: Government Printing Office,
   1976). A critical evaluation of the DIA and military intel-
   ligence is provided in Patrick J. McGarvey, CIA: The Myth and
   the Madness (Baltimore: Penguin Books, Inc., 1972), especially
   Chapters V, VI, and VII. Also see Marc B. Powe and Edward E.
   Wilson, The Evolution of American Military Intelligence (Fort
   Huachuca, AR: The U. S. Army Intelligence Center and School,
   1973).

10. Joseph A. McChristian, The Role of Military Intelligence, 1965-
    1967 (Washington: Government Printing Office, 1974).

11. Glen B. Infield, Unarmed and Unafraid (New York: Macmillan
    Company, 1970) and John W. R. Taylor and David Monday, Spies
    in the Sky (New York: Charles Scribners Sons, 1972).

12. George W. Goddard with DeWitt S. Copp, Overview: A Life-Long
    Adventure in Aerial Photography (Garden City, NY: Doubleday,
    1969).

13. Phillip J. Klass, Secret Sentries in Space (New York: Random
    House, 1971).

14. Wilhelm F. Flicke, War Secrets in the Ether (Laguna Hills, CA:
    Aegean Park Press, 1977).

15. Alfred Vagts, The Military Attache (Princeton, NJ: Princeton
    University Press, 1967).

16. Jeffrey M. Dowart, The Office of Naval Intelligence: The Birth
    of America's First Intelligence Agency, 1865-1918 (Annapolis,
    MD: Naval Institute Press, 1979) and James R. Green, The First
    Sixty Years of the Office of Naval Intelligence (Washington:
    American University, 1963).

17. Joseph C. Goulden, Truth Is the First Casualty: The Gulf of
    Tonkin Affair -- Illusion and Reality (New York: Rand McNally,
    1969).

18. Trevor Armbrister, A Matter of Accountability: The True Story
    of the Pueblo Affair (New York: Coward-McCann, Inc., 1970).

19. Stedman Chandler and Robert W. Robb, Front Line Intelligence
    (Washington: Infantry Journal Press, 1946), Robert R. Glass
    and Phillip B. Davidson, Intelligence Is for Commanders
    (Harrisburg, PA: Military Service Publishing Company, 1948),

Irving Heymont, <u>Combat Intelligence in Modern Warfare</u> (Harrisburg, PA: Stackpole Company, 1960), Edwin E. Schwein, <u>Combat Intelligence: Its Acquisition and Transmission</u> (Washington: Infantry Journal, 1936), and Elias Carter Townsend, <u>Risks: The Key to Combat Intelligence</u> (Harrisburg, PA: Military Service Publishing Company, 1955).

20. David Kahn, <u>The Codebreakers: The Story of Secret Writing</u> (New York: Macmillan, 1967), James Bamford, <u>The Puzzle Palace</u> (New York: Houghton Mifflin, 1982), and U. S., Senate, Select Committee to Study Governmental Operations with Respect to Intelligence Activities, <u>Hearings. Volume 5. The National Security Agency and Fourth Amendment Rights</u> (Washington: Government Printing Office, 1976).

21. Ray S. Cline, <u>Secrets, Spies and Scholars: Blueprint of the Essential CIA</u> (Washington: Acropolis Books, Ltd., 1976) and Cline, "Policy Without Intelligence," <u>op. cit.</u>

22. Sanford J. Ungar, <u>FBI</u> (Boston: Little, Brown and Company, 1976), Harry and Bonaro Overstreet, <u>The FBI in Our Open Society</u> (New York: W. W. Norton, 1969), and U. S., Congress, Senate, Select Committee to Study Governmental Operations with Respect to Intelligence Activities, <u>Hearings. Volume 6. Federal Bureau of Investigation.</u> (Washington: Government Printing Office, 1976).

CHAPTER 4

The Central Intelligence Agency

Introduction

The CIA is the focal point of the U.S. intelligence community. It is the one community component that most Americans and many foreigners can name. Indeed, few of those outside of the community can even identify any of the other units of the U.S. intelligence apparatus. Although Chapter 3 indicates that the CIA is neither the largest nor the most expensive community structure, "The Company" is the most important component in terms of public opinion, coordination of intelligence production, and some forms of collection and operations. It is the most visible structure, it is formally responsible for coordinating the activities and output of the community, and it conducts activities that no other community structure does. This salience means that a detailed look at the CIA is necessary for even an introductory understanding of the U.S. intelligence community.

The CIA is similar to any large bureaucracy in many ways.[1] Its internal organization has changed since its creation in 1947, responding to both external and internal pressures. Its importance to foreign policy making has fluctuated with the perspectives of the foreign policy elite and the changes in international affairs. Its Director is nominated by the President and appointed by the Senate, and he reflects the President's view of the intelligence community. Internally, it is characterized by a hierarchical organization, routinized communications channels, and standard operating procedures that are associated with all governmental agencies. However, the CIA, like the rest of the intelligence community, differs from most governmental units in some key respects.

The number of presidential appointees is far more limited in the CIA than in most federal bureaus. Normally, only the Director of Central Intelligence (DCI) and the Deputy Director of Central Intelligence (DDCI) are chosen by the President, although this limitation is traditional rather than statutory. Unlike the majority of governmental structures, most of the high-ranking officers of the CIA are intelligence, and usually CIA, veterans. The rationale for this practice is that the CIA must remain apolitical in order to maintain an objectivity that is essential to unbiased analysis. The philosophical assumptions of representative government demand that any public structure whose activities are necessarily secret must not become a tool of any one group in society, but rather must serve the nation, conceived as a single entity. This notion is analyzed more extensively in

45

Chapter 5, but the important point to note in this discussion is that the CIA is run by intelligence professionals, not "lateral entry" appointees of any one president or political party.

Another basic feature of the CIA is that its most notable activities -- clandestine operations that include assassination attempts, coups d'etat, governmental, economic, and social "destabilizations," and support for regimes and organizations that are friendly to the United States -- constitute only one part of all CIA functions. Thus, the focal point of the intelligence community is the CIA and the focal point of the CIA is the Directorate of Operations. While this focus may be useful for some purposes, it is oversimplistic and dysfunctional if we are trying to understand the intelligence community and its problems and prospects. Chapter 3 indicated that the intelligence community is far more than just the CIA. Likewise, the CIA is far more than just the Directorate of Operations.

CIA Structures and Functions

The internal composition of the CIA changes from time to time. While it is not always in a state of flux, no description of CIA structures is immutable. Likewise, the activities or functions of the Agency expand and contract over time, especially in terms of emphasis. The salience of any one part of the CIA will vary with the importance of the activity it performs. So, the internal dynamics of the CIA are not rigid. Despite this dynamic character, certain structures and functions are constant, although names and jurisdictions may change. Our review of the CIA will focus on these "constants," using the most current structural titles. It is based on the organization shown in Chart 4.1.[2]

There are three types of structures in the CIA. One of these is the office of the Director of Central Intelligence (DCI). This individual, like the Deputy Director (DDCI), is selected by the President with the concurrence of the Senate. A second type of structure is the staff units of the CIA. These offices are necessary for any bureaucracy and their functions are procedurally similar to those governmental units that are not intelligence-oriented. A third type of structure is the functional or line units of the CIA, the Directorates. Each of these is headed by a Deputy Director who almost always is an intelligence veteran. While the functions performed by the Directorates distinguish the CIA as the main element of the intelligence community, it is important to appreciate the contributions of the office of the DCI and the staff units.

DCI.[3] The Director of Central Intelligence has two basic responsibilities. One pertains to the entire intelligence community

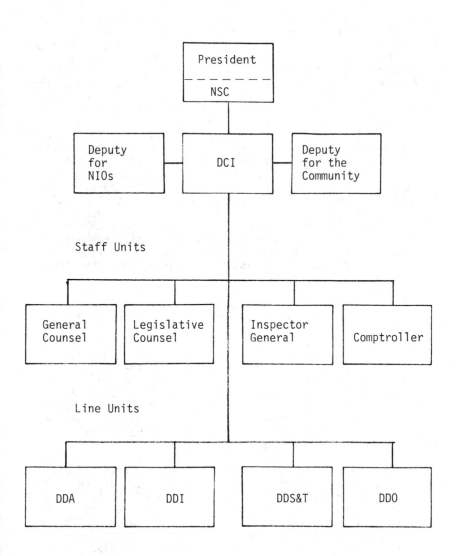

Chart 4.1 The Central Intelligence Agency

and the other pertains only to the CIA. In both instances, the DCI is ultimately responsible for the intelligence process and product. The arrangement of the DCI's office reflects the attempt to simultaneously centralize and coordinate the work of the entire community and direct and manage the CIA. The DCI has several deputies that assist in these various tasks. One of these is the Deputy Director of Central Intelligence. This individual serves as the complement to the DCI in the basic division of responsibilities between the community and the CIA. Normally, the DCI will adopt a community-wide perspective and the DDCI will focus on running the CIA. However, since both of these individuals work out of offices on the elite seventh floor of CIA headquarters in Langley, Virginia, it is impossible to neatly divide their daily tasks. Both inevitably become spokesmen for the entire community and both must be concerned with the activities and performance of the CIA. By custom one of these individuals has a civilian background while the other is from the military. Also, at least one of these has an extensive background as an intelligence professional. Within the DCI's office, the DDCI is the most important assistant. However, two other individuals are also crucial to the DCI.

The Deputy for National Intelligence Officers is responsible for managing the production of reports and analyses by the 12 National Intelligence Officers of the CIA.[4] These dozen people are career intelligence veterans whose collective expertise covers a wide range of geographic and issue areas. While they tend to conduct their respective studies individually, the Deputy coordinates their efforts and serves as a linkage between these "wise men" (used in the generic sense, since women have occupied the position of National Intelligence Officer or NIO) and the DCI's office. NIO reports are observations and conclusions based on experience and scholarship and are intended to be topical and timely inputs to the policy-making process.

The Deputy for the Intelligence Community serves the DCI by maintaining the desired relationship with the rest of the intelligence apparatus.[5] Chapter 3 indicated the diversity of the community and suggested the inevitable bureaucratic rivalry that is our concern in Chapter 5. Since the DCI is head of both the community and the CIA, his loyalty is necessarily divided and is often suspect by the other community members. The Deputy for the Intelligence Community is responsible for assisting the DCI in overcoming this suspicion. This individual is the link between the CIA and the rest of the community, and the position demands integrity, pragmatism, and a strong personal loyalty to the DCI.

Staff Units. These CIA offices perform the necessary administrative functions common to any large governmental organization. While the activities of the CIA staff units must necessarily

48

reflect CIA concerns, the rationale for them is similar to that which necessitates their counterparts in any federal agency.

The General Counsel provides legal services for the CIA. Given the diversity of CIA activities, the General Counsel is involved in virtually all aspects of the law. For instance, because the CIA operates "cover" commercial enterprises that seek to maintain a legitimate business appearance, the General Counsel must be skilled in corporate law, tax law, estates and trusts, and other branches of the law. Of special importance in recent years is the protection of classified information about the CIA from dissatisfied or disaffected former employees. A number of books and articles have been written in the past decade that reveal the organization and activities of the CIA. The General Counsel has been given the responsibility for preventing the publication of those materials which, in the view of the CIA, the DCI, and the President, would be detrimental to the U.S. national security. The success of these efforts has varied, depending on the merits of each individual case, legal and judicial interpretations, and the availability of alternative publishing avenues.

The Legislative Counsel acts as the link between the CIA and Congress. The legality of some CIA activities has been a problem since the Agency's creation. The National Security Act of 1947 and the CIA Charter of 1949 are vaguely worded and ambiguous regarding the statutory limits of CIA operations. This has caused uncertainty about the propriety of CIA actions, and congressional committees can interpret the existing statutes broadly or narrowly. This flexibility may be useful as an abstract principle of constitutional law, but it has resulted in confusion regarding permissible activity. Throughout the 1950s and most of the 1960s, the relevant Senate and House committees interpreted the statutes loosely and even encouraged an active and aggressive CIA. In the 1970s, and especially in 1975, both the Senate and the House conducted exhaustive investigations into past CIA conduct and chose, retrospectively, to apply more stringent interpretations of the statutes. The Legislative Counsel is the CIA unit that is responsible for determining what the CIA is legally permitted to do, and its task is a complicated but vital one. It is important to note that most CIA employees endorse the official CIA request for a new, comprehensive, and definitive charter that will ameliorate the legal uncertainties. The position of the Legislative Counsel is that such a charter must not restrict the CIA from activities that are traditionally part of intelligence (including espionage) work and that clandestine operations must be among the options of a major power in international affairs.

The Inspector General (IG) serves as an internal policeman. This office is responsible for investigating the official activities of CIA personnel and for reporting to the DCI any improprieties or appearances of impropriety. The Inspector General is a part of nearly every department, bureau, or agency of government, but it is particularly relevant to the CIA. Because the Agency necessarily conducts some of its activities in secret, its employees must be trustworthy. If they are engaging in improper or illegal activities, the trust cannot be maintained. The importance of this principle is illustrated by the consequences of the 1975 congressional investigations referred to above. Those investigations revealed some questionable and a few illegal operations by the CIA. One result of those revelations was a drop in employee morale and an exodus from the Agency of the most disaffected people who felt their patriotic reasons for working for the CIA had been compromised. The Inspector General serves as a kind of ombudsman for these kinds of people. If an employee questions the propriety of a task he or she is assigned, the Inspector General can offer an opinion. In this way, the IG attempts to prevent transgressions and restrain those whose aberrant behavior would destroy the trust that is a necessary justification for the CIA, a secret part of a representative government. While it is important to note that the Inspector General is not responsible for internal security or counter-espionage, it is the burden of the IG to have CIA personnel remain, in the words of a former DCI, "honorable men."

The Comptroller is responsible for the financial maintenance of the CIA. This office must prepare a budget annually and oversee the expenditure of funds. Since the budget is a classified document, and because the principle of unvouchered funds that began with the OSS continues, the CIA Comptroller must be characterized by integrity and a familiarity with the needs and goals of the various parts of the CIA. The Comptroller is almost always an intelligence professional, as are most of the high-ranking staff personnel. This individual must have the trust of the heads of the various parts of the CIA, and he or she must maintain an objective and comprehensive perspective of the CIA as a single entity.

These four offices emphasize the legal and financial basis for the substantive CIA activities. The General Counsel represents the Agency in courts of law, the Legislative Counsel serves as its legal liaison with Congress, the Inspector General provides an opportunity for self-policing, and the Comptroller determines the internal allocation of budgeted funds and future budgetary needs. Each is essential to the continued existence of the CIA and their importance cannot be overstated. However, it is the functional units that define the activities of the CIA as a unique governmental agency. There are four of these functional units, known as Directorates, as shown in Chart 4.2 (Interestingly, the Soviet KGB also calls its functional units Directorates.) Each is headed by a Deputy Director who reports directly to the DCI.[6]

Directorate of Administration. The head of this unit is the Deputy Director of Administration, and both he and the unit are known as DDA. Chart 4.2 shows the main parts of DDA, which provides the personnel, equipment, and other forms of support required by the other Directorates. Indeed, DDA used to be called the Directorate of Support. A look at the main units of DDA will reveal its diversity.

The Office of Personnel is responsible for recruitment, retention, and release of CIA personnel. While the Office of Personnel determines Agency employment needs from the units it serves (mainly the other Directorates), it conducts the preliminary interviews, constructs and administers the various types of entrance examinations, and screens out those applicants who clearly are not suited for Agency employment. Obviously, the CIA is not an equal opportunity employer. Many of its positions require specific skills and aptitude. Prospective employees are subjected to rigorous testing, including a polygraph or "lie detecting" examination, psychological and mental tests, and, in some cases, tests of physical fitness. Because the jobs in the CIA are so varied, there is no one profile that results in acceptance. However, applicants must demonstrate a commitment to the principles of American government and a sense of pragmatic nationalism. Other attributes that often are crucial to CIA employment include foreign language aptitude, a willingness and even desire to live and work abroad, and the ability to work in a thoughtful and imaginative way with a minimum of supervision or direction. The Office of Personnel maintains offices in major cities in the United States and also sends recruiters into areas not served by local offices.

The Office of Security is responsible for the physical security of CIA buildings and personnel. The headquarters building in Langley, Virginia, is continually subjected to various kinds of security checks, as are CIA and other U.S. buildings abroad. The CIA has strict regulations regarding the disposition of documents, memoranda, and even carbon paper. Offices are checked on a daily basis to ensure that safes are locked, that no classified material is exposed, that "burn bags" and shredding machines have been used when appropriate, and,in general, that the work of the CIA is secure from those who do not "need to know." The Office of Security also conducts periodic electronic "sweeps" of CIA buildings to make sure that no transmitters or other devices have been secreted to gain access to classified conversations. James McCord, who led the Watergate team of

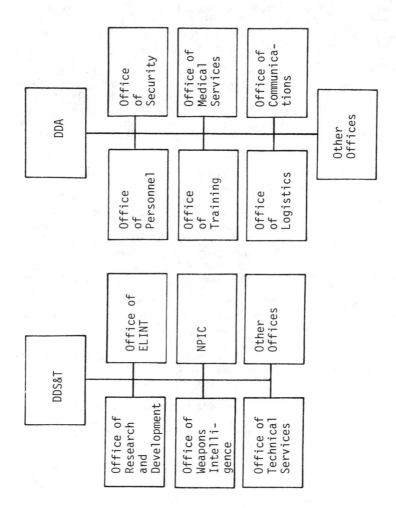

Chart 4.2 The CIA Directorates (DDA and DDS&T)

infiltrators, had once served as the head of the Office of Security, although it is important to note that he had resigned from the CIA some time before he became involved in that venture.

The Office of Training has the task of providing some CIA employees with their requisite skills. Not everyone who joins the CIA requires the services of this office. For instance, lawyers, accountants, computer operators, and language experts are employed because of their demonstrated expertise and require no training in their professions. However, the CIA does perform what one former employee has called "peculiar service," and the Office of Training is responsible for teaching those peculiarities. Such training includes the arts of espionage and counterespionage, how to interpret photographs taken from space, coding and decoding messages, how to "run" an agent, how to organize and conduct paramilitary operations, and the intricacies of psychological warfare. In many cases, the training takes place at Camp Peary in the Virginia countryside, at a place called "The Farm." Here, those employees who are going abroad receive instruction in how to perform their respective tasks. For these individuals whose lives will be in some degree of jeopardy, perhaps the most important lesson is how to maintain their covers. Another important part of this training is instilling in these people the knowledge that while the U.S. and the CIA cannot publicly acknowledge their employment if their covers are "stripped," the Agency will attempt to repatriate them should they be incarcerated abroad. This is usually accomplished through a "spy swap," and this type of transaction is a routine part of the sometimes byzantine world of espionage. Knowledge of this principle is a vital morale factor for those "in the field."

The Office of Medical Services provides health care for CIA employees, although "health" in this case has a somewhat unique interpretation. This office includes a dispensary in the headquarters building that administers to routine health problems. However, its more unusual "health services" pertain to the stresses of working with classified material that requires secrecy. The psychological strains on Agency personnel are a concomitant of these stresses. This is true for headquarters as well as field personnel. The combination of risk, secrecy, and psychological estrangement resulting from living a "cover" often requires medical and mental help, and many field personnel require the assistance of Medical Services. However, even those who work at Langley are not immune to the pressures resulting from the analysis of data crucial to the national security. Alcoholism and divorce are two areas of particular concern to Medical Services. Since the CIA wants to retain its personnel in order to have continuity and expertise, Medical Services endeavors to solve these personal health problems internally so that its personnel will be able to discuss those problems without compromising classified information.

The Office of Logistics is the supply center of the CIA. Although it supplies the ordinary office needs of any organization, such as desks, light bulbs, and typing paper, its most important function is supplying CIA operatives abroad. For years the CIA has had a reputation among national intelligence services of being able to deliver more goods faster to any place in the world than any other intelligence service. The Office of Logistics maintains a large warehouse complex along the west bank of the Potomac, south of Arlington National Cemetery. While critics argue that these warehouses contain enough weapons to equip a reputable military force, the Office of Logistics is also able to supply a variety of material for the conduct of information gathering under diverse circumstances. It is important to note that Logistics does not design or create this material, since its task is to stockpile, transport, and deliver the paraphernalia requested and approved for use in the field.

The Office of Communications is a vital part of DDA. In one respect it is perhaps the most important DDA unit. This office provides the linkage between headquarters and the field. Much of the raw information which is collected abroad is transmitted through the Office of Communications. Once known by its OSS name of Cable Secretariat, this office maintains a worldwide network of transmitters and receivers so that Langley can function as the center of CIA operations wherever they are. The Office of Communications has a close working relationship with the Office of Logistics as well as other Directorates. Naturally, virtually all of the communications are in some code or cipher, and this makes the work of this office especially sensitive. One basic principle of the intelligence profession is that speed and accuracy of information transmission is vital to success. This principle makes the work of the Office of Communications particularly demanding.

There are other offices in DDA, including Finance and Computer Support. Together with those discussed above, they offer the support functions for the other Directorates. While DDA differs somewhat from administrative parts of other bureaucracies, the other three CIA Directorates have no counterparts outside of the intelligence community. This is especially true of the Directorate of Science and Technology.

Directorate of Science and Technology. Like all other aspects of society and government, the CIA has adjusted to the remarkable progress of science and technology in this century. Indeed, the invention and development of technological devices has greatly increased the speed and accuracy of the intelligence process. The importance of science and technology to the intelligence process is demonstrated in the activities of the Directorate of Science and Technology, DDS&T.

The Office of Research and Development not only conducts its own research efforts, but also monitors research and development in other countries. It maintains an active interest in scientific conferences and findings and follows the progress of technological developments abroad. Its personnel are extremely "high quality," with many holding graduate degrees. Its primary focus is in the field of espionage technology, and especially in PHOTINT. The U-2 and SR-71 "spy" planes, satellite information gathering, and other technological devices for the collection and recording of data have been created by the Office of Research and Development.

The Office of ELINT, previously called the Office of Electronics, is responsible for improving electronic surveillance. Like the Office of Research and Development, the Office of ELINT works closely with other members of the intelligence community to develop and maintain the most advanced and sophisticated equipment for information gathering. This cooperation, especially with Naval Intelligence and the NSA in the case of the Office of ELINT, allows the CIA to share in the process of transforming electronic information into intelligence.

The Office of Weapons Intelligence is responsible for monitoring the number, quality, and types of weapons possessed by various countries. Data collected by various means is assessed by the Office of Weapons Intelligence to determine the capabilities of potential friends and foes. For instance, wars in the Middle East provide information on how well U.S.-made weapons perform against Soviet-made weapons, and the 1982 Falklands War revealed the potential vulnerability of some surface vessels to certain air-to-sea guided missiles. While all data on weapons technology is important to the Office of Weapons Intelligence, its main task is to monitor and assess the nuclear capability of the Soviet Union. The strategic nuclear forces of the USSR have been a major concern of U.S. intelligence ever since the Soviets have progressed to the rank of superpower in large part because they have acquired the ability to fight a nuclear war. Thus, it is vital for U.S. intelligence to know the capability of the USSR in this special field of weapons. The analysis of Soviet nuclear forces is not exclusively done by the DDS&T Office of Weapons Intelligence, but this office does serve as the primary civilian intelligence component for the assessment of the military potentials of foreign nations, including the USSR.

The National Photographic Interpretation Center, NPIC, is the focal point of PHOTINT processing.[7] This office of DDS&T is responsible for reviewing and analyzing photographs, primarily those taken by satellites and spy planes. This activity permits the intelligence community to update its knowledge of other nations, and while the analyses usually reflect marginal changes, occasionally NPIC reveals evidence that results in dramatic political consequences. For instance, in the Cuban Missile Crisis of 1962, U.S. decision makers were able to know when the Soviet missiles could be launched against U.S. targets because of the skill of NPIC interpreters. These individuals had been studying photographs of Soviet missile-site construction for years and were able to inform the President and his advisors on the daily and hourly development of the missile sites. The status of the missile-site construction was the vital piece of information required by the U.S. decision makers, and NPIC played a crucial role in assisting them. This is an example of how the intelligence process sometimes works without human spies or espionage agents. However, since DDS&T serves the entire CIA, it does have a connection to the world of espionage, primarily through its Office of Technical Services.

Like many parts of any intelligence organization, the Office of Technical Services is a title that sounds important but is not very revealing. In this case, the title refers to espionage or clandestine activities that require special types of equipment or techniques. The equipment provided by Technical Services includes special cameras for taking photographs with little light, disguises, passports, identification cards, and other documents, weapons with various unique capabilities, and miniature devices for transmitting, amplifying, and recording conversations. Technical Services is intended primarily to support HUMINT operations, and consequently it often devises its equipment for specific individuals and specific tasks. While it performs the more fanciful activities of DDS&T, it is important to remember that most of the work of DDS&T supports more mundane input to the intelligence process. Much of that input goes to the Directorate of Intelligence.

Directorate of Intelligence.[8] The Directorate of Intelligence, DDI, produces most of the intelligence documents that are disseminated to the rest of the community and to the NSC and the President. Its offices, like those of DDA and DDS&T, are organized according to functional concerns. DDI is staffed primarily with individuals whose background and training emphasize research and analysis.[9] Its activities have been compared to the world of academia, and, indeed, it employs a number of people with graduate academic credentials. When a national security crisis threatens U.S. interests, DDI is responsible for timely and accurate analyses and estimates. For instance, it was the Deputy Director of Intelligence who first explained the photographs of Soviet missile installations in Cuba to President Kennedy in October, 1962. However, most of the work of DDI is of a more routine nature, reflecting its main task of estimating and anticipating trends and changes abroad. While some of the data supporting these analyses is collected covertly, much of it is taken from "open" sources such as newspapers, broadcast media, and academic and other

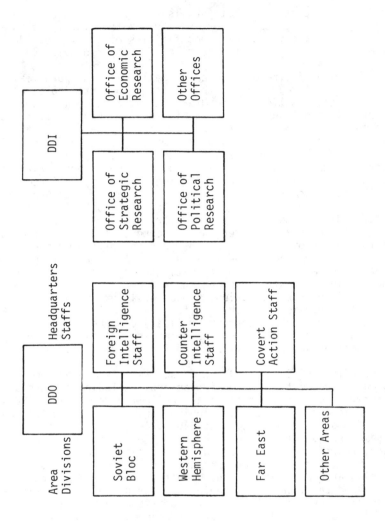

Chart 4.2 The CIA Directorates (DDI and DDO)

57

journals and reports. The main skills that DDI personnel have are foreign language proficiency, research methodology, and analytical training. The functional specificities of the various DDI offices reflect the areas of expertise of DDI personnel.

The Office of Strategic Research deals with the potential of other countries to wage war, although its fundamental concern is the nuclear capabilities of the USSR, China, and, to a lesser extent, Britain and France.[10] Strategic Research constantly evaluates satellite photographs, radar and telemetry data, and other information gathered by technological means. It also reviews statements by foreign leaders and scientists as well as published reports that may be useful in making conclusions about strategic concerns. Like all DDI offices, Strategic Research is forced to make its estimates on the bases of both fact and conjecture. Its task is like trying to solve a puzzle in which some pieces are well defined in terms of shape and color, but the entire picture is unknown. The puzzle solver must proceed on the basis of guesses about the number of pieces, the configuration of the missing pieces and their relationship to the known pieces, and the basic picture the puzzle reflects. This "guestimating" requires great expertise in and knowledge of strategic weapons and doctrines plus a proven ability to integrate the various pieces of information into a reasonable conclusion. Another factor that complicates the work of Strategic Research is that the military components of the intelligence community also produce estimates and analyses, and disagreement between the military and the CIA views is inevitable.

The Office of Economic Research scrutinizes the economies of every major and most minor foreign actors, including nations and such international organizations as the Common Market and OPEC. Its economic concerns are wide-ranging and include financial postures and prospects, production capabilities, and commercial arrangements and philosophies. For example, Economic Research produces reports and estimates on Soviet grain production, OPEC oil reserves, the current and projected strength of various currencies around the world, the expected effects of business mergers, and the impact of changing weather patterns on agricultural growing cycles. The work of Economic Research tends to be less crisis-oriented than most other DDI components because of the nature of economic and commercial activity, but its reports can have significant consequences. For instance, a National Intelligence Estimate produced in the late 1970s suggested that, under continued circumstances prevailing at that time, the USSR would be forced to enter the foreign market for oil and other petroleum goods by 1985. The fundamental change by the Soviet Union from a net exporter to a net importer of oil would necessitate new policies by the United States and other countries, and prior knowledge of the change would permit making policies to anticipate and accommodate the changes. The vast majority of research done by the Office of Economic Research results in similar reports that assist in long-term economic planning rather than the management of economic crises.

The Office of Political Research is the political-governmental counterpart to Strategic Research and Economic Research. Like them, it emphasizes trends rather than immediate effects, although it does produce analyses of expected and unexpected changes in political systems and regimes. Its concerns are as wide-ranging as the field of political science and include such diverse topics as campaigning practices, styles and effectiveness of public administration, judicial and legal systems, types of political parties and their relevance to different political systems, the prerequisites and prospects for political development, regime succession and its consequences, the relationships of culture and ideology to political change and governmental stability, terrorism, and the relationships between domestic policy and foreign policy. Political Research surveys all of the political-governmental entities in the world, but focuses on the Soviet Union, China, and the less developed countries of the Third (and Fourth) World. Its basic task is to alert policy makers to probable or possible changes, but it may be assigned the added responsibility of suggesting appropriate U.S. responses to those changes. It is important to note that final policy decisions are made by the foreign and national security policy elite, which may include the DCI. Political Research, like all of DDI, transforms information into intelligence, but the policy decisions based on that intelligence are made by the President and his immediate advisors. Obviously, the intelligence produced by DDI can and often does greatly influence the policy choices, and this has been a significant problem of CIA-White House relations in the past, as we will see in Chapter 6.

There are several other units in DDI that are important in the production of intelligence reports. The Foreign Broadcast Information Service monitors radio and television programs around the world. It is especially concerned with news programs, and its summaries and analyses of broadcasts are disseminated throughout the intelligence community and to other parts of the federal government. The Office of Geographic and Cartographic Research maintains files of maps and geographic data and monitors changes in topography, climate, and other geographic data. The Collection Guidance and Assessment Staff reviews the accuracy, reliability, and utility of data collected for use by DDI and is concerned with both overt and covert collection means. The Office of Current Intelligence generates estimates and analyses of events and situations of topical interest to both policy makers and the general intelligence community. It produces daily and other periodic reports as well as evaluations of crises.

The Directorate of Intelligence is designed to provide policy makers with the knowledge of events that they need to make and conduct the affairs of the United States abroad. While its major task is to supply an unbiased and objective view of the world, it may also suggest or recommend policies based on its assessments. This is the traditional role of an intelligence service and it is a vital part of the policy-making process. Without adequate intelligence, policy success becomes a matter of luck and the probability of policy failure becomes great. The extent to which DDI provides adequate intelligence has been a matter of dispute, and we examine the arguments in Chapter 5. The important point is that the work of DDI is a legitimate and necessary activity of the intelligence community. The questions of legitimacy and necessity are more controversial in the case of the Directorate of Operations.

Directorate of Operations.[11] Because the mere existence of the Directorate of Operations is the most controversial aspect of the intelligence community, we will examine legitimacy and necessity in greater detail in Chapter 6. DDO, also known as Clandestine Services, has three basic missions: Espionage, counterespionage, and covert action. To coordinate and fulfill these missions, DDO has three staffs of individuals with professional expertise in their respective areas. In addition to these three DDO staffs, the work of the Directorate of Operations is divided into various geographic Area Divisions since DDO conducts most of its work overseas.

The Foreign Intelligence Staff is concerned with espionage, especially HUMINT or the collection of information by human means. This is the popular notion of what the CIA does and is commonly referred to as "spying." The Foreign Intelligence Staff monitors current espionage techniques and results and oversees major espionage efforts. Its function is to provide direction and guidance rather than select specific espionage "targets" or missions, although it may assist in some particularly important cases of espionage. Espionage is a profession and is conducted according to certain principles of pragmatism. The Foreign Intelligence Staff assesses these principles as they relate to current HUMINT missions and seeks to improve the quality of the collection of information by espionage "agents." Another function of the Foreign Intelligence Staff is the evaluation of HUMINT. Evaluation of information is a constant activity throughout the process of converting information into intelligence. HUMINT in particular requires evaluation by trained experts who are familiar with the specifics of the collection, including the agents, the targets, the social, historical and psychological setting, and concurrent collection efforts in the same functional area and geographic locale. Information is evaluated according to perceived accuracy and reliability. This evaluation process is necessary because of the vast amount of information collected. The relevant information (i.e., accurate and reliable) must be distinguished from the relatively useless or even dysfunctional information. This process can only be done by people who have had experience in the collection of such information.

The Counterintelligence Staff is primarily concerned with protecting U.S. intelligence, and especially the CIA, from "penetration" by foreign intelligence services, especially the Soviet KGB. Counterintelligence, or counterespionage, is a field that emphasizes suspicion and doubt. It assumes, with good reason, that rival intelligence services are constantly attempting to acquire intelligence about our intelligence service. Since much of the work of the CIA involves sensitive material, and because that material often concerns the national security of the United States, it is necessary to protect our secrets from the espionage efforts of others. While critics have characterized the Counterintelligence Staff as paranoids, it is inevitable and perhaps even necessary that these individuals regard everyone as a potential "mole" or "double agent" who appears to be working for the CIA but in reality is relaying information to the intelligence service of another country. The focus of the Counterintelligence Staff is on the headquarters personnel and is not confined to those assigned to DDO. The purview of the Counterintelligence Staff extends across administrative boundaries since a mole working in DDI, DDA, or DDS&T is as much a threat as one in DDO. This extensive jurisdiction, combined with the natural suspicion of the Counterintelligence Staff, occasionally results in disputes about administrative control and bureaucratic "turf," but the necessity for an active and vigilant counterespionage unit is an accepted principle of the intelligence business.

The Covert Action Staff is responsible for planning and executing the most popularized and more glamorous activities of the CIA. Covert action implies undertakings against foreign governments or other actors (terrorist organizations, political parties, individuals, etc.) which the U.S. government, and especially the President, wants to deny undertaking. The propriety of covert action is a continuing debate and we will examine it in Chapter 6. Regardless of its philosophical or even practical merits, covert action is an option all presidents have had. The Covert Action Staff is responsible for ascertaining the chances of success of such operations and determining the various costs, including financial requirements, the threat of possible exposure of the operation as U.S.-inspired, and the effects of failure should the operation not succeed. The staff is basically a study group that assesses the positive and negative features of proposed covert actions and makes recommendations to the Deputy Director of Operations who then advises the DCI.

Each of these staffs does most of its work at CIA headquarters in Langley, Virginia. They are relatively small and highly experienced and, as the term "staff" implies, they assist the Deputy Director of Operations (DDO) in the three major functional areas

61

of intelligence, counterintelligence, and covert action. They serve as a link between the DDO and the individuals who serve abroad, or "in the field." The actual foreign operations are organized according to geographic areas, and include Europe, the Western Hemisphere, the Far East (with an emphasis on the Peoples' Republic of China), the Near East (including North Africa), Africa (south of the Sahara Desert), and, most important, the Soviet Bloc (USSR and Eastern Europe). Each of these Divisions is separated into Stations. The Station is the basic administrative unit of Area Divisions, and each Station is managed by a Station Chief. Frequently, a Station will coincide with a country (e.g., Greece and Great Britain). In some cases several small or relatively unimportant countries may be combined into a single Station, and in a few instances a large and very important country may be subdivided into several Stations.

Each Station Chief has a staff which includes intelligence, counterintelligence, and covert action experts plus administrative assistants. The main purpose of a Station is the collection of information, especially by human means. This is done by means of agent networks, or, as they are known in the CIA, reseaux. (Reseau is French for "network.") The individuals that comprise a reseau and the principles of creating and maintaining a reseau are the subject of the Appendix. It is important to note at this point that Americans rarely "spy." Instead, the head of each reseau, known as a Case Officer, normally recruits local citizens to conduct the actual espionage, for reasons explained in the Appendix.

The Director of Operations is not solely responsible for the clandestine operations conducted by the U.S. intelligence community. As we have seen, a number of agencies, bureaus, and departments of the U.S. government are involved in obtaining information that other nations seek to protect. However, because DDO involves HUMINT to much greater extent than the other units, and because it is assigned covert action operations on occasion, it has become a main focal point of critics of the CIA and the entire intelligence community. The debate over the propriety of the United States engaging in such activities as attempted assassinations, economic "destabilizations," and coups d'etat has become only one of the major problems confronting the intelligence community.

NOTES

1. Lyman B. Kirkpatrick, Jr., The Real CIA (New York: Macmillan Company, 1968).

2. U. S., Senate, Select Committee to Study Governmental Operations with Respect to Intelligence Activities, Final Report. Book IV. Supplementary Detailed Staff Reports on Foreign and Military Intelligence (Washington: Government Printing Office, 1976), p. 102 and Victor L. Marchetti and John D. Marks, The CIA and the Cult of Intelligence (New York: Alfred A. Knopf, 1974), pp. 84-85.

3. Stafford T. Thomas, "On the Selection of Directors of Central Intelligence," Southeastern Political Review, IX (Spring 1981).

4. U. S., Senate, Select Committee, Final Report. Book IV. Supplementary Detailed Staff Reports, op. cit.

5. Ibid.

6. Marchetti and Marks, op. cit.

7. Glenn B. Infield, Unarmed and Unafraid (New York: Macmillan Company, 1970).

8. Ray S. Cline, Secrets, Spies and Scholars: Blueprint of the Essential CIA (Washington: Acropolis Books, Ltd., 1976).

9. J. Richards Heuer, Jr., ed., Quantitative Approaches to Political Intelligence: The CIA Experience (Boulder: CO: Westview Press, 1978).

10. Lawrence Freedman, U. S. Intelligence and the Soviet Strategic Threat (Boulder, CO: Westview Press, 1977).

11. Harry Rositzke, The CIA's Secret Operations: Espionage, Counterespionage, and Covert Action (New York: Reader's Digest Press, 1977), Theodore Shackley, The Third Option: An American View of Counterinsurgency Operations (New York: McGraw-Hill Book Company, 1981), Peer De Silva, Sub Rosa: The CIA and the Uses of Intelligence (New York: New York Times Book Company, 1978), Marchetti and Marks, op. cit., and Paul W. Blackstock and Frank L. Schaf, Jr., Intelligence, Espionage, Counterespionage, and Covert Operations: A Guide to Information Sources (Detroit: Gale Research Company, 1978).

CHAPTER 5

Internal Problems

Introduction

Since its permanent inception in 1947, the intelligence community has been the subject of debate and controversy in America and around the world. It has been criticized from a variety of perspectives and it has been the focus of inquiry by a number of diverse societal elements, including the three branches of government, the press, public opinion, and interest groups. All of this attention has resulted in problems for the intelligence community. One set of problems concerns the internal dynamics of the community. Here we are concerned with understanding how the community functions and what some of the inherent limitations on its capabilities and potential are.

Internal Problems

These are problems that result from the structural and personnel characteristics of the intelligence community. Accordingly, one set of internal problems centers on the ability of the intelligence community to coordinate its efforts, both administratively and in terms of its products, while another group of internal problems concerns the factors of leadership and morale which are particularly important to the intelligence community.

Administrative and Product Coordination.[1] The salient structural characteristic of the intelligence community is its diversity. Chapter 3 illustrated the number of units that comprise the community and suggested that these units are a community only in the technical sense that they all share a common goal. In reality that goal is interpreted or perceived differently by each of the units. Indeed, even within any one unit there may be disagreement on the appropriate emphasis the various meanings of the term "intelligence" should have. For instance, the different activities pursued by the CIA's Directorates of Intelligence and Operations result in divergent views of what is most important in the intelligence process and what products the community should emphasize.

The structural diversity of the U.S. intelligence community precludes consistent administrative coordination. Each of the main bureaucratic units either is independently strong, as in the cases of the CIA and NSA, or is an integral part of an independently strong agency or bureau, such as the DIA, the three service components, INR, and the Internal Security Division of the FBI. This independence results in a bureaucratic parochialism, with each unit defending its administrative jurisdictions against

65

encroachment by the others. It means that the community is characterized by both functional and allocational rivalry, since each unit attempts to expand the tasks it performs and its percentage of the budget allocated to perform those tasks, although there are limits to this rivalry. For instance, the main espionage effort has always been performed by the CIA and the main domestic counterespionage operations have always been done by the FBI. However, just as it is impossible in practice to precisely delineate domestic politics from foreign policy, most intelligence activities are performed by more than one unit of the community, and there is competition between the units. Despite this competition and partially offsetting the overlap of functions and activities, there is a degree of cooperation, such as the provision of diplomatic "covers" by the State Department for some CIA employees serving in foreign countries.

The intense competition between intelligence community components means that control, direction, and guidance of the U.S. intelligence effort are usually lacking. While major covert actions are reviewed and monitored by the National Security Council, the White House, and the Special Action Group, the routine, daily activities are characterized by a lack of overall coordination. This may be inevitable with any large group of individuals charged with performing a variety of functions.

A related problem of coordination concerns the impact of technology on the collection and processing of intelligence. Approximately 95 percent of all information which enters the U.S. intelligence process is acquired by technological means -- ELINT, PHOTINT, SIGINT, and COMINT. Since machines can operate more continuously and reliably than humans and because all of the departments, bureaus, and agencies of the community use technology as the main method of information gathering, the community has the problem of an information glut. As the technology becomes more sophisticated, more information enters the process. Thus, part of the problem is quantitative. There is an ever-increasing amount of data to process. The other part of the "information glut" problem is qualitative. The various pieces of information have different levels of importance. This means that more expertise is required to assess or evaluate the increasing amounts of data. The result is that the parochialism that characterizes the administrative aspects of the community is also manifested in the collection and analysis stages of the intelligence process.

The intelligence community is uncoordinated in most of its activities. A major ramification of this situation is that its products, including NIEs and periodic reports, frequently are uncoordinated also, or, when they do reflect consensus, are too ambiguous to be of great use to Administration policy makers. The problem of conflicting intelligence assessments is a particularly difficult one for any Administration to solve. The problem has several interrelated aspects. Each part of the intelligence community produces its own analyses. Each analysis is based on information acquired by one or several of a variety of methods, which are different from sources that serve as the basis for other, competing analyses. Each analysis reflects the variety of values, perspectives, and goals of the producing unit. Thus, the decision makers frequently are confronted by an uncoordinated intelligence product, characterized by conflicting intelligence analyses based on a variety of acquisition methods and a variety of implicit perspectives. The purpose of the community is to produce intelligence for policy making and implementation. While some of its products serve this purpose, many do not because they do not present options or consensus, but rather reflect disagreements within the community.

Compounding this problem is the frequent lack of expertise by the policy makers. Since extensive experience in intelligence is rarely an asset in electoral politics, most elected and appointed high-ranking Administration officials cannot appreciate the background of conflicting intelligence analyses and recommendations. This appears to be an increasing problem with the election of Washington "outsiders" who rely heavily on the advice of their immediate political colleagues. If the President has little practical experience in foreign affairs and is primarily influenced by advisors who are mainly concerned with the partisan political effects of Administration decisions, uncoordinated intelligence products will result in policy decisions based on factors other than intelligence. Indeed, even when presented with a coordinated intelligence product, an inexperienced group of policy makers whose main focus is the domestic political consequences of its decisions is likely to alter or ignore the advice of the community. So, while the community may speak with many voices, it may also be addressing an unreceptive ear, or one that only hears what it wants to hear. This was certainly the case during the 1960s.

Throughout the Vietnam War, the intelligence community was divided over the issues of how to fight the war and the prospects of success. The analyses and estimates produced by the CIA's Directorate of Intelligence consistently took the position that the struggle was basically a political-social one and consequently DDI opposed transforming it into a large-scale military struggle. DDI analyses argued that a military victory over the Viet Cong (VC) and North Vietnamese Army (NVA) was not possible, given the inability to create and maintain a popular regime in South Vietnam, the popularity of North Vietnam's leader, Ho Chi Minh, his autocratic regime, the lack of support for our effort by our major allies, the lack of sufficient domestic U.S. support for a prolonged, costly war effort, and the desire to limit the basic objective to preventing a communist victory in South Vietnam. These views were in direct opposition to the conclusions of

military intelligence. The DIA and the individual intelligence
components of the three services argued that the situation was
primarily a military problem and that the problem could be solved
by military means. Their perspective was that the VC and NVA were
basically military organizations and that they could be defeated
on the battlefield if we were sufficiently committed and motivated
to achieve victory. While these two conflicting analyses pre-
dated direct U.S. military involvement, the intelligence community
debate became especially acute in the mid-1960s.

The military intelligence view prevailed over CIA's analyses,
for several reasons. Lyndon Johnson, despite a long tenure in the
Senate, was inexperienced in foreign affairs and had a rather
simplistic view of the complicated politics of international relations. The military analyses were more persuasive to him since
they were less qualified and presented the problem as a contest
of wills, which appealed to Johnson's world view. A second reason
was that Johnson's advisors, especially Dean Rusk and Robert
McNamara, were more inclined to accept the military perspective
and were more skeptical of CIA analyses, in part because of the
lingering embarrassment of the Bay of Pigs fiasco, which they
blamed primarily on poor CIA intelligence product. A third
factor was the lack of vigorous leadership of the CIA in the
crucial period of 1964-1965. The DCI at this time was Admiral
Raborn, who had virtually no intelligence community background
before his appointment and who appears to have had little influence on Administration decisions.

Another reason the military view prevailed was that, while
DDI was producing intelligence reports that conceived the problem
as a political-social one, the CIA's Directorate of Operations
was heavily committed to a variety of covert actions of paramilitary nature. While these two activities were not incompatible
they appeared that way to Administration officials. In contrast,
the military presented reports and estimates that reflected an
internal consistency. Finally, military intelligence was accepted
because of the preponderant weight it has in the community. Chapter 3 illustrated that military intelligence is larger and more
expensive than the civilian components, and therefore, it often
is viewed as more important or significant to the inexperienced
consumers of intelligence. This brief analysis shows that the
consequence of conflicting, uncoordinated intelligence products
is often a policy choice that is based on factors that may be
only marginally related to the substance of the analyses themselves. However, this does not necessarily mean that a coordinated product is always useful to substantive policy making.

The intelligence community does sometimes produce estimates
and analyses that reflect a consensus. These reports are distil-
lations of various views from throughout the community. The
problem with these products is that compromise is necessary to

achieve unity. The result of this compromise usually is a product that is highly qualified and tentative in both its rationale and conclusions. This means that the policy makers, who often are inexperienced and therefore require and prefer definitive and simple policy options, must proceed as if they were sophisticated and knowledgeable about the intricacies and nuances of international relations. These coordinated intelligence products can be very useful to the experienced practitioner, but are not very helpful to the consumer who does not understand the unique features that characterize foreign policy making and implementation. Consensual reports require not only the ability to appreciate the subtleties of their various applications, but also an awareness of intracommunity politics that enables the consumer to "read between the lines."

The dilemma of product coordination is a complex one that involves community politics, consumer experience and receptiveness, and the style, logic, and substance of the product. Separate analyses from various community members inevitably conflict and usually present policy makers with reasonably clear choices, which may be unrelated to the intelligence upon which the product was based. Coordinated, consensual reports rarely present clear choices unencumbered by qualifications, which may result in policies that require an expertise normally not always found in contemporary Administrations. Neither alternative is completely satisfactory, nor does a satisfactory resolution to this dilemma seem both feasible and practical. A partial solution would be to have a DCI who could command the allegiance of the entire intelligence community. This suggests another major set of internal problems.

Morale and Leadership.[2] The individuals who comprise the intelligence community are not a typical group of governmental employees. While some community employees perform tasks that are similar to those performed in any large bureaucracy, such as administration, computer programming, congressional liaison, and legal advocacy, the majority of community personnel are chosen only after careful scrutiny and assessment. The screening procedures include a detailed investigation of a prospective employee's application, not only for security and counterintelligence reasons, but also to ascertain the suitability of the applicant for the position. Interviews are extensive and the testing procedures are designed to make sure that the individual is suited by education, experience, and personality for the job. Because the tasks performed by the community are so varied, the kinds of individuals employed by the community are extremely diverse, ranging from mercenaries who live a life of constant danger to academics who contemplate and analyze. Regardless of the working environment, all community employees are influenced by the secrecy of their work and most feel that they are performing tasks that are critical to the national security of the United States. Compared to other

69

governmental units, intelligence personnel are usually more intelligent and more sensitive. No community member is an "equal opportunity employer." None is strictly subject to affirmative action policies or guidelines. The work of the intelligence community and the need for security mean that high employment standards can be set and maintained. Another factor that contributes to the maintenance of these high employment standards is the unusually high ratio of applicants to job openings.

There are many reasons why people aspire to careers in intelligence. Community units incorporate these motivations in their recruitment interviewing and testing processes. Since these employers can and must be highly selective, they can establish the criteria for acceptance. The four main criteria are patriotism and a commitment to liberal, democratic values, a heightened sense of integrity, a commitment to developing and maintaining skills that often are unique and arcane to the intelligence profession, and the feeling of loyalty that derives from membership in an exclusive and secret organization. Another factor that characterizes most candidates, and that is understood and appreciated by community employers, is the desire to be involved in the aura of the secret, exciting, and sometimes dangerous world of intelligence. While most intelligence work is characterized by none of these aspects, the myth of intelligence persists, fostered by popular spy fiction and occasional media revelations of covert actions. All of these motivations are part of the recruitment profile, and the interviews and tests prior to employment are designed to insure that the community is staffed by competent, confident people who are committed to their tasks because they recognize the importance of those tasks.

It is important to note that monetary reward is not a factor of employment that is stressed by the community. Although the CIA and other community agencies, departments, and bureaus offer the usual governmental compensations, the emphasis is on career orientations. Because the background security checks are so costly and since the work frequently entails classified material, it is vital that employees be dedicated to the intrinsic factors of intelligence work and give the job a higher priority than they give to personal financial reward. A related consideration is that individuals who work primarily for money are more susceptible to overtures by counterespionage agents of other nations' intelligence services. Financial inducements are the primary means of penetrating an intelligence organization, so great efforts are made to insure protection against this threat. Individuals who indicate that money is a significant factor in employment are usually not accepted.

The result of this emphasis on commitment to the country and the job is a community of individuals who require effective leadership and high morale in order to succeed. Because they work for mostly unselfish reasons, these people need constant reassurance and evidence that "someone cares." If leadership is lacking, morale suffers because the employees feel their efforts are not being recognized. In this sense, the intelligence community is a unique bureaucracy. It has no "natural clientele" other than the President and the NSC. If its leaders, and especially the DCI, are ineffective in maintaining a close and positive relationship with the primary intelligence consumers, employees become less motivated and the quality of the product inevitably declines. Consequently, unlike most other public agencies, the work of intelligence community members is greatly influenced by their leadership, and especially by the type of DCI appointed by the President.

The basic factor that determines the leadership-morale relationship is the intelligence background of the DCI. To a group of people committed to and indoctrinated in the intelligence business, "outsiders" are suspect. If the DCI is an intelligence professional, he is more likely to command the respect of the community in the various councils of government. Conversely, if the DCI has little or no intelligence experience, he is likely to be viewed with skepticism by the community as someone who does not understand the particular needs and aspirations of the intelligence profession. Indeed, "outsiders" are often given the task of changing the structure, emphases, and ranking personnel of the community and especially the CIA. These administrative and functional changes may or may not be justified, but since the CIA in particular is a presidential organ, the President's perspectives on intelligence are the primary factor in the activities and behavior of the intelligence bureaucracy.

The variation in community and especially CIA morale is primarily a function of the type of DCI chosen by the President. The four basic tasks any DCI performs involve administration of the community and particularly the interrelationships between the CIA and its military counterparts, policy advice on matters of foreign and national security policy, policy implementation of decisions made by the White House and NSC, and satisfying certain partisan political needs of the DCI's main patron, the President. While each DCI inevitably discharges all of these duties, the President and his immediate advisors usually indicate which of these four tasks is their primary concern.

Morale tends to deteriorate most under administrators, as the case of James Schlesinger best illustrates. He served a very brief tenure (February-July, 1973) as DCI under President Nixon and National Security Advisor Kissinger. The White House had become displeased with both the intelligence products and the results of covert activities under Schlesinger's predecessor, Richard Helms. Consequently, Schlesinger's mandate was to restructure the CIA, which he proceeded to do with dispatch. In

71

the process, a number of the most venerable CIA careerists were fired, and many of those who remained were uncertain and doubtful regarding their careers and the future of the U.S. intelligence community. Generally, administrators are chosen because the President wants changes and those changes almost always have a negative effect on morale, especially when instituted by "outsiders" who do not begin with the confidence of the intelligence professionals.

Policy advisors tend to produce the highest levels of morale. Since they are part of the inner circle of the policy-making elite, they are in the best position to represent the community's views forcefully and successfully. Advisors usually are intelligence professionals who best understand and empathize with the sensitivity and motivations of community personnel. The best example of an advisor was Allen Dulles, who served as DCI from 1953 to 1961. During part of this period, 1953-1958, his brother, John Foster Dulles, was Secretary of State. The Dulles brothers dominated foreign policy decisions during this time, so the DCI had exceptional policy "clout" in the Eisenhower Administration. Also, Dulles was an intelligence professional, having been one of the architects of America's post-World War II intelligence community. Another factor that enhanced morale under Dulles was the public and media acceptance of the importance and legitimacy of intelligence work, especially covert action aimed at communism. Dulles was able to develop and sustain a favorable climate for the intelligence professionals and to secure an important role for them. Together with his understanding of the unique and sensitive psyche of the intelligence officer, these factors resulted in a high level of morale and self-esteem among community personnel.

Under policy implementors, morale tends to be dependent upon the ability of the DCI to effect a significant role for intelligence in policy decisions. While implementors may appear to be part of the policy-making elite, their primary duty is to carry out the decisions of that elite. If the implementor-DCI has input regarding the role of the community or its parts in policy decisions, morale tends to be high. If, however, the implementor is relegated to the role of merely implementing the directives of the White House, morale tends to be weakened. The experience of Richard Helms illustrates this point. Helms, a career intelligence officer, served as DCI from 1966 to 1973. In the early part of his tenure, he was able to influence some policy decisions although he was never a close White House advisor. Vietnam was the focal point of foreign policy, and while he was unable to have CIA estimates and analyses prevail over the military intelligence products, he did secure a prominent role for the community in the paramilitary aspects. As a result, morale in CIA's DDI began to weaken as the views of that unit were disregarded, but morale in the Directorate of Operations remained high since it continued to have an active part in the prosecution of the war. In his later years as DCI, Helms was completely excluded from policy making and became totally subservient to the Nixon-Kissinger White House. Morale suffered accordingly throughout the CIA.

Partisan choices are made for a variety of reasons, some of them unrelated to intelligence. A disaffected wing of the President's political party may require evidence of Administration recognition, an individual with great electoral potential may need visibility and enhanced credentials, or a close personal advisor to the President may need a strong bureaucratic base from which to serve. Normally, partisan choices do not have an extensive background in intelligence, and thus are not likely to have a positive effect on the morale of a relatively exclusive fraternity with special needs. However, since partisan choices usually have a great deal of influence, based on the reason(s) suggested above, this type of DCI has the potential to increase community morale. The best recent example of a partisan choice was George Bush. Although he had some foreign policy experience, Bush knew very little about intelligence or the community when he was appointed. His Senate confirmation hearings were characterized by a concern that his appointment was temporary, and that he was going to use it to further his own political future. As a result of these doubts and his own inexperience, the community regarded this with a degree of skepticism. It was feared that the community was being used as a political pawn rather than perceived as an important and vital unit of government. Actually, morale improved under Bush, even though he was DCI for only one year. The three major factors that accounted for this unexpected result were his importance in the Republican Party, which at that time controlled the White House, the relative weakness of President Ford, who had succeeded Nixon and who was perceived by many as a caretaker until the 1976 elections, and, perhaps most significant, Bush's patience and his genuine desire to learn about intelligence. Bush retained most of the professional staff and made few changes. Externally he was an adequate spokesman for community concerns in the councils of government. So, morale under partisan choices need not suffer, despite the circumstances that accompany their appointments.

The leadership-morale factor is especially important to intelligence professionals. They are motivated by a sense of service and self-effacement, and if they are directed by individuals who understand their motivations and the peculiarities of their profession, morale is high, products are generated professionally, and activities are performed with greater competence. Conversely, Directors who fail to empathize or recognize the special needs and demands of an intelligence career and who do not demonstrate a forceful attitude toward the community environment (e.g., the President and NSC, Congress, and the media) are

73

unlikely to enjoy the respect of the community and almost certainly will experience a decline in morale and its concomitant, poorer community performance.

Conclusion

Every Administration must deal with these problems. Bureaucratic and production coordination are extremely difficult to achieve given the parochialism the various community components manifest and the administrative strength and security each of them has. While there are some incentives to cooperate, the community is basically a confederation with a weak central point (the DCI) and strong individual units that can resist many of his directives. Without a strong and clear commitment by the Administration, coordination of the intelligence community will be sporadic and minimal. However, the results of a highly coordinated community might negate the value of several different sources and perspectives that result in policy options. The dilemma between too much or too little coordination is a problem that cannot be solved, but can only be managed, and it requires an adroit, pragmatic, and experienced President and DCI.

The leadership-morale problem is another concern that relates to the inner working of the community. The type of DCI chosen by the President and the performance and policy making influence the DCI has are factors that greatly affect community morale and, ultimately, performance. The intelligence profession attracts individuals that require periodic if not continual recognition of their contributions. They need recognition that what they are doing is important, and that they are doing it well. While this is true of everyone, it is especially characteristic of intelligence work. When intelligence morale declines and its products and activities deteriorate, the national security posture is weakened. Thus, morale is an important problem and it is affected by the type of leader chosen as DCI. But presidents have a number of concerns in making their choices, and morale is only one of them. Other intelligence community problems are related to the environment of the community and the relationships between the community and its environment.

NOTES

1. Joseph A. McChristian, The Role of Military Intelligence,
    1965-1967 (Washington: Government Printing Office, 1974),
    Lyman B. Kirkpatrick, Jr., The U. S. Intelligence Community:
    Foreign Policy and Domestic Activities (New York: Hill and
    Wang, 1973), U. S., Congress, House, Select Committee on
    Intelligence, Hearings. Part 2. U. S. Intelligence Agencies
    and Activities: The Performance of the Intelligence Community
    (Washington: Government Printing Office, 1976), Harold L.
    Wilensky, Organizational Intelligence: Knowledge and Policy
    in Government and Industry (New York: Basic Books, 1967),
    Edmund S. Hawley, "The Administration of the Intelligence
    Community," Monograph on National Security Affairs (Provi-
    dence, RI: Brown University, 1976), and Harry Howe Ransom,
    The Intelligence Establishment (Cambridge, MA: Harvard Uni-
    versity Press, 1970).

2. Stafford T. Thomas, "On the Selection of Directors of Central
    Intelligence," Southeastern Political Review, 9 (Spring 1981),
    William E. Colby, Honorable Men: My Life in the CIA (New York:
    Simon and Schuster, 1978), Allen W. Dulles, The Craft of
    Intelligence (New York: Harper and Row, 1963), and Thomas
    Powers, The Man Who Kept the Secrets: Richard Helms and the
    CIA (New York: Alfred A. Knopf, 1979).

CHAPTER 6

Domestic Problems

Introduction

The relationship of the intelligence community to its environment is dominated by one basic characteristic. There are many critics, some of them hostile, and few consistent and powerful supporters. The intelligence community, unlike most bureaucratic entities, has no "natural clientele," whose continued existence and prosperity depends on the bureau's success. The community and especially its main component, the CIA, may at times have defenders, but those proponents frequently either lack influence or offer only qualified support. The community serves the "national interest" of the United States, and that ambiguous and abstract term has as many different meanings as those who define it. In transforming "national interest" into a concrete and specific policy, the perceptions and perspectives of the individual policy makers determine its meaning. Thus, even the consumers of the various intelligence products disagree about the validity, accuracy, and quality of intelligence. Those who are not consumers but who have an impact on policy making tend to be even more critical of the intelligence community since they are denied its products and are therefore skeptical of its policy contributions. This environmental relationship is exacerbated by the inability of the community to publicly and convincingly defend and explain its actions. For reasons of security, especially the security of its intelligence sources and methods, the community response to critics, usually made by its main spokesman, is either "No comment" or a response that is necessarily ambiguous and usually unsatisfactory to the questioner.

The CIA is the focal point of the U.S. intelligence community. It is the one community component that most Americans and many foreigners can name, and, indeed, is the only component that most "outsiders" can even identify. One consequence of this salience is that the CIA (also known as "The Company" to "insiders") receives most of the criticism for intelligence "failures" as well as most praise for the more infrequently publicized successes. (Many intelligence professionals, especially those in the CIA's DDO and its Counterintelligence Staff, feel that any publicized action or operation is a failure.) When U.S. intelligence fails to predict world events such as the Iranian revolution and subsequent seizure of the U.S. embassy in Teheran, it is the CIA that is blamed. Similarly, when secret U.S. involvement in foreign events becomes public knowledge, the CIA often is the target for charges of impropriety and/or ineptitude. The increase in aggressive investigative journalism, together with fewer restrictions on the secrecy of governmental activities, has meant that the CIA has become the prime governmental unit that critics of America's foreign and national security policies focus upon.

The CIA also is the main community beneficiary when the U.S. intelligence apparatus is praised. This happens far less often than revelations of questionable or inefficient activities, since no intelligence organization wants to admit it is succeeding. Such indications of success would necessarily be followed by changes by the target of the successful operation, thereby negating the success. So, when an intelligence organization is succeeding, it cannot reveal its operations. Nor is it wise to acknowledge past successes, since that would alert current and future antagonists to methods of operations and thus make intelligence collection much more difficult. This reluctance to admit to foreign operations explains the standard CIA reply to inquiries, "No comment." This should be interpreted literally, since either a positive or negative response, given truthfully, would do a disservice to U.S. intelligence and would be useful to others who are the presumed object of the inquiry.

The problems that result from this situation were succinctly summarized by President John Kennedy at the dedication ceremonies of the CIA's headquarters in 1961, when he pointed out that the successes of intelligence remain unknown while its failures are widely publicized. The effects of this dilemma on morale are analyzed in Chapter 5. The external effects are no less significant and extensive. The various external observers perceive the intelligence processes and products differently and are motivated by different concerns. Part of the total environment is the major domestic institutions that affect foreign and national security policies, including the White House and the National Security Council, Congress, and the media and public opinion. The other set of environmental institutions or factors, which are addressed in Chapter 7, are found in the international arena and consists of allies and adversaries. However, regardless of the particular environmental institution, there is one fundamental philosophical problem that pervades all of the processes and activities of the CIA and its community bretheren.

Secrecy in an Open Society[1]

The main assumption of an open, pluralistic, democratic society is that the people must be adequately informed about the policies and conduct of their government in order to choose their representatives. The main assumption of any intelligence apparatus is that security must be maintained in order to render the intelligence product useful. These two assumptions are diametrically opposed in the United States. The U.S. is one of the most open societies, with a vigorous media whose investigatory liberties are protected by the Constitution, a public that is not well-informed but is nonetheless very opinionated concerning foreign affairs, and a liberal persuasion that often emphasizes individual rights over societal needs. The political culture of the U.S. is characterized by a distrust of big, centralized, powerful government that is unresponsive to its citizens. This distrust frequently focuses on those organs of government that must operate in secrecy or not operate at all, the intelligence community and especially its most salient part, the Central Intelligence Agency.

The intelligence profession requires security, almost by definition. Without it, rival intelligence organizations could easily determine America's policies in advance, allowing their respective governments to capitalize on those policies. If all of the activities, methods, and sources of intelligence were revealed for domestic consumption, they would also be revealed for foreign consumption. Since there are adversaries in the world who strive to weaken if not eclipse the United States, revelation of our intelligence is self-defeating. Thus, the dictates of an open society are incompatible with the dictates of an effective intelligence community.

The recent history of the intelligence community has reflected a continuing attempt to reconcile this dilemma. The following diagram illustrates various answers to the question of the proper role of intelligence in an open society.

Complete Openness	Skepticism	Acceptance	Complete Secrecy

At one extreme are those who advocate complete openness. This position favors public revelation of the community's activities, open debate of its foreign and domestic operations, and treating the community like other governmental agencies. Its advocates include a mixture of extreme civil libertarians, world federalists, and foreign elements hostile to the United States. If its goals were achieved, the intelligence community would cease to be an effective or useful part of the United States government, since its activities could not be conducted and its products would not enhance government policies. Advocates of this view argue that America should be a free, open society with a government that is responsive to citizen demands. As the only part of the government that is legally secure from intense citizen and media scrutiny, the intelligence community is the focal point of those who advocate this position. The principle that summarizes this extreme is that if America cannot be a completely free and open society, it is inconsequential how successful it may be in its foreign affairs. This is essentially an isolationist world view since it disregards any consideration of hostility or threat from abroad in favor of efforts to improve conditions of liberty at home.

The other extreme views the world as a hostile and antagonistic setting that requires unity, vigilance, and a continual concern with America's international primacy. The advocates of this view argue that other nations seek to weaken or even subjugate the United States, that those nations are firm in their resolve, dedicated to their primary task, and strong in their capabilities. This challenge to the existence and preeminence of America must be met by all necessary means. The principle that guides these people is that domestic concerns must be subordinated to international exigencies. This implies that secrecy must be complete, not only to insure that our policies are formulated and implemented successfully, but also to permit necessary clandestine military, political, economic, and social operations against foreign governments. This position reflects the notion that failure to respond to foreign threats will result in the demise of America, which will render the question of civil liberties moot. This is essentially a globalist world view that suggests no citizen restraint on government, complete trust in our political executives, an extremely optimistic perception of America's (and the intelligence community's) capabilities, and an ethnocentric attitude that American policies are justified and pragmatic regardless of the views and aspirations of other peoples. Its advocates include extreme political conservatives and some religious fundamentalists.

Neither of these extreme views has ever been popular. They are rejected by the vast majority of citizens and politicians, probably because they are so extreme and would result in the elimination of one of two principles that most Americans value, either the continued existence and importance of America in world affairs or a viable, responsive, and representative government. In comparison to other major countries, Americans are more pragmatic than ideological, and therefore most citizens tend to favor a less extreme position on the question of the necessary and appropriate role of secrecy in an open society. Because pragmatism often determines public opinion on this issue, historical events often have an impact on attitudes and opinions about the intelligence community. Concomitantly, that public opinion frequently affects the activities and productivity of the community. Recent shifts in public attitudes about the CIA illustrate the impact of such historical events.

Until the era of the Vietnam War, most Americans supported a strong and active foreign policy and endorsed the necessity for a vigorous intelligence effort to support that policy. The Cold War that characterized U.S.-Soviet relations presumed a hostile adversary that was aggressive in many ways and had to be resisted. While not accepting the need for extreme secrecy, the security needs of the intelligence profession were acknowledged, as long as they did not intrude significantly on domestic political activity. Another factor that contributed to this attitude was the success of the principal intelligence organization during this period. While the 1961 Bay of Pigs fiasco presaged the end of popular "peacetime" support for the CIA, the CIA achieved its assigned tasks in Italy (1948), Iran (1953), and Guatemala (1954). It also successfully countered most attempts by the Soviets to destabilize friendly regimes elsewhere. The CIA, led by the avuncular and slightly mysterious Allen Dulles, was regarded as a successful, glamorous, dynamic, and appropriate tool to meet the new kind of threat posed by the USSR. As long as Americans perceived their country's mission as the leader of a non-Communist world besieged by Soviet-inspired adversaries, secrecy in an open society was accepted as a necessity, although absolute secrecy was regarded as neither necessary nor tolerable. The CIA, the media, Congress, and presidents contributed to this climate of opinion. The CIA selectively revealed its successes to enhance its image without severely jeopardizing its ongoing operations or methods. The press reflected a positive view of CIA activities, at times creating myths about how, why, and where the Agency did its work. Congress generally endorsed the work of the Agency and frequently chose to disregard its congressional oversight functions. Presidents used the Agency and other community members when other governmental bodies may have been more appropriate. Thus, until the Vietnam War era, the intelligence professionals (and especially those in the CIA's clandestine services directorate) were generally lionized and regarded as legitimate and vital agents of the American government.

The Vietnam War profoundly affected America in a pervasive and multi-faceted way. It had numerous consequences, but perhaps the most important was a greatly increased ability and willingness to question the authority and legitimacy of the U.S. government. This was especially true of the presidency and the executive branch. The media changed its view of American government and in many cases adopted an adversarial, antagonistic, and dubious attitude about official governmental statements and policies. This shift had a resultant impact on public opinion, which reflected doubt about the veracity of many government pronouncements. This attitude of skepticism was reinforced by the Watergate episode.

Just as America's direct involvement in Vietnam was ending and there was a reasonable prospect for an increase in the public's perceptions of governmental legitimacy, the revelations of Watergate became known. The main effect of this episode was a further weakening of public support for and faith in government. The fact that Congress played a key role in revealing the Watergate transgressions helped to focus public opinion on the presidency and the executive branch. By 1975, the combination of Vietnam and Watergate resulted in a perceived need, at least by the media and a large portion of Congress, to reassess America's domestic and foreign policy priorities. The question of secrecy in an open society was raised again, and the shift in public mood was manifested in a different general attitude toward the intelligence community and its most important member.

In 1975 the community was the object of intense public scrutiny unparalleled in history. No country had ever subjected its secret organs of government to such open and extensive review. The Church Committee in the Senate, the Pike Committee in the House, and the White House's Rockefeller Commission held lengthy hearings and did voluminous research into past activities of the intelligence community. The congressional committees conducted their business openly and publicly, adopted an adversarial, accusatory, and investigative approach, and, perhaps inevitably and irresistibly, dramatized its proceedings. It based its hearings on allegations of illegal and/or inappropriate behavior by intelligence officials through the years. It rarely acknowledged any legitimate reasons for clandestine operations and operated under the assumption that most clandestine or secret activities were indefensible. In world view, the congressional committees, and especially their chairmen, came close to the complete openness extreme. It is important to note that they were joined in this attempt to reveal past activities by a press that emphasized investigatory reporting and a tendency to judge government against a set of ideals, a non-elected President anxious to avoid the mistakes of his predecessor, and a Director of Central Intelligence who was willing to comply with congressional requests for testimony and information. While the Rockefeller Commission had a less diffident attitude and a more conciliatory approach, its conclusions were similar in substance, if not emphasis, to those of the Church and Pike Committees.

The 1975 inquiries uncovered few clear violations of the law, in part because the laws pertaining to the intelligence community were so vaguely worded. However, all of the investigating bodies concluded that there had been improprieties in community behavior, especially in the area of clandestine operations. The consequences of these investigations were varied and profound, and they indicated that the public view of secrecy in an open society had shifted to one of skepticism. The work of the community was no longer automatically accepted as necessary and legitimate. Instead, it was questioned and regarded as often inconsistent with America's values. In abstract terms, intelligence was equated with spying, espionage, destabilization of other nations' economies, coups d'etat, and assassinations of foreign leaders. Since these activities were associated with the same hubris of globalism that many people associated with our involvement in Vietnam, they were rejected as unnecessary, unwise, and unworthy aspects of American foreign policy and as inconsistent with and contrary to the ideals that America should project abroad.

The most important consequence of the 1975 investigations was legislation designed to make the secret parts of the U.S. government more open. Under the Freedom of Information Act, individuals could obtain government records that heretofore had been classified. While this permitted citizens to correct inaccurate and potentially damaging information about themselves, it was so exhaustive in its openness that espionage agents operating against the United States on behalf of foreign interests could determine government knowledge of their activities. Under the Hughes-Ryan Act, eight different committees of Congress and their staffs had to be informed before any covert action was undertaken by the intelligence community, which meant that over 1,000 people would know of such actions in advance. Additionally, if any committee member disapproved of the covert operation, he or she could reveal it publicly without punishment. These attempts to open government and make it more responsive to the people and their representatives were reactions to the frustrations of a losing and ultimately unpopular effort in Southeast Asia and to the illegal and excessive activities that characterized Watergate.

Attitudes toward the proper role of the intelligence community and the acceptance of secret activities by parts of the government are conditioned by many factors. Historical events and eras have a significant affect since they provide the foundation for world views. The historical pattern is that when Americans perceive a major foreign threat, the fortunes and importance of the intelligence community increase, but when Americans are unconcerned about foreign threats or ventures, intelligence is neglected or severely restrained. Thus, the public attitude toward secrecy in an open society varies and to a great and fundamental extent is a function of the public's view of America's role in the world. Other factors that affect public acceptance of or support for an active intelligence community are related to this basic factor.

Different administrations use the community in different ways. In Chapter 5, the consequences for the community of different types of Directors are analyzed. Since the President chooses his Director, the Chief Executive's view of the world and America's place in it affects the operations and activities of the

83

the community. President Eisenhower endorsed an extremely active
CIA under Allen Dulles. President Kennedy used the CIA discrimi-
nately as an implement of foreign policy, but was skeptical of
some of its products, especially in the period following the
Bay of Pigs invasion of April, 1961. President Johnson's focus on
Vietnam caused him to disregard most CIA analyses in favor of those
of the Defense Department, but he used the Agency extensively in
covert actions in Southeast Asia. President Nixon and his chief
foreign policy advisor Henry Kissinger also rejected most CIA
analyses as too liberal in perspective, and Nixon sought to use
the CIA in impractical covert operations and in illegal domestic
actions. President Carter greatly decreased the use of covert
action and de-emphasized HUMINT as a means of collection. Thus,
the world view of the President is an important factor in determining what, how, when, and where the intelligence community operates.

Media attitudes are another critical factor in understanding
the limits of community behavior. In the Cold War period before
Vietnam, the press was generally supportive of community activities. Newspapers and weekly news magazines often praised the CIA
and emphasized its successes. The clandestine service in particular was mythologized and honored. The community was presented as
America's primary weapon in the Cold War. In the post-Watergate
era of investigatory reporting, the media generally have been un-
supportive and often antagonistic to the community. Little
attempt has been made to separate product from process or legitimate activity from illegitimate. While media skepticism of and
antagonism toward government is a general characteristic of this
period, it is especially evident in the case of the intelligence
community. This relationship, together with the increased pressures of competition within the media and a continuing public
fascination with the business of espionage and intelligence, means
that stories about the community are always "news" regardless of
their veracity, relevance, or importance.

Congress also affects the role of the intelligence community
in American society. The Church and Pike Committees were part of
a general trend throughout the 1970s that reflected greater attention by Congress to the substance, style, and conduct of American
foreign policy. While it continues to manifest these concerns,
recent legislation by Congress indicates a modest shift toward
greater acceptance of the community and its necessary security.
The Freedom of Information Act has been modified in an attempt
to eliminate some of its provisions, such as those that require
disclosure of certain intelligence sources and methods. Also,
the Intelligence Identities Protection Act of 1982 prohibits the
willful disclosure of the identities of U.S. intelligence operatives.

This shift in congressional mood may be accompanied by shifts in public opinion, the presidency, and perhaps even the media. It is doubtful that the shift will ever return to the limits of the Cold War. The more fundamental question is whether the community can meet the expectations that accompany such a shift.

Acceptance of a more significant role for the community embodies the expectation that the community can do those things expected of it. In the late 1970s the community, and especially the CIA, was inhibited by presidents, Congress, the media, public opinion, and even by its own admissions of past improprieties and occasional illegalities. Covert action virtually ceased, HUMINT collection was de-emphasized, many foreign intelligence sources ("assets") stopped reporting for fear they would be exposed in the media, allied intelligence services decreased their cooperation for the same reason, and community morale suffered greatly. One major result was that intelligence products at times were not satisfactory. The best example was the Carter Administration's surprise over the Iranian revolution and the seizure of the U.S. embassy in Teheran. This was a classic "intelligence failure" since some intelligence analysts were correct in their predictions of these events. Much of this particular failure can be attributed to poor product coordination, discussed in Chapter 5. However, the failure also is attributable to the trend in the late 1970s to "get out of the spy business." The decision by President Carter and his DCI, Stansfield Turner, to de-emphasize HUMINT resulted in fewer reports concerning the mood of the Iranian people and their attitudes toward the Shah.

Such intelligence failures are inevitable if there is neither public nor presidential support for the intelligence community. Even with such support, the community has problems of administrative and product coordination, discussed in Chapter 5. The intelligence professionals also have another set of problems to confront. These problems are in the international arena and involve relations with allies and struggles with adversaries.

Conclusion

The intelligence community is a unique institution of American government. In order for it to operate successfully, its budget, many of its officers, its operations, some of its products, and much of its internal functioning must remain secret. Public disclosure of these factors would negate its effectiveness, especially in the area of clandestine services. This basic security requirement conflicts with the fundamental precept of an open, democratic, representative government, the right and the need of public knowledge of government institutions. This is the basic domestic problem of the intelligence community. Without adequate secrecy and security, any national intelligence apparatus is virtually worthless. But without adequate public knowledge and awareness of the intelligence apparatus, such an institution represents a potential threat to civil rights and liberties. Possible solutions to this dilemma range from total secrecy to total openness, with neither extreme representing a satisfactory solution.

America's experience with a permanent and substantial intelligence community has been to shift from acceptance of extensive secrecy to rejection of extensive secrecy. The critical factors that explain this shift have been perceived threat to America from abroad, the relationship between the media and the community, the role played by Congress in foreign and national security policy making, and the perceptions by the President and White House of America's world role and the community's utility in performing that role. While these factors can be separated analytically, in reality they are interrelated and constitute the domestic environment of the community. What the community or its components does at any one time is determined by this domestic environment. In the period before Vietnam and Watergate, the factors supported active and extensive foreign operations to implement U.S. policy abroad. Since the mid-1970s, the domestic environment has curtailed such operations as Americans have reassessed their relationships to government and especially to its foreign policy.

This basic shift has had a fundamental impact on the ability of the community to act in the foreign environment. The conduct of foreign operations requires a degree of stability, regardless of the form those operations have. Whether the task is covert collection (espionage), counterintelligence or counterespionage, or covert action, America's "secret agents" need support that can only be effective if it is consistent. An analysis of the community's foreign environment will indicate the validity of this conclusion.

NOTES

1. Richard H. Blum, ed., <u>Surveillance and Espionage in a Free
Society: A Report by the Planning Group on Intelligence and
Security to the Policy Council of the Democratic National
Committee</u> (New York: Praeger, 1972), Judith F. Buncher, <u>et al</u>,
eds., <u>The CIA and the Security Debate: 1971-1975</u> (New York:
Facts on File, 1976), Peer De Silva, <u>Sub Rosa: The CIA and
the Uses of Intelligence</u> (New York: New York Times Book
Company, 1978), <u>Monograph on National Security Affairs, The
CIA: Past Transgressions and Future Controls</u> (Providence, RI:
Brown University, 1975), James A. Urry, "Secrecy and the
Intelligence Community," <u>Monograph on National Security
Affairs</u> (Providence, RI: Brown University, 1976), U. S.,
Congress, House, Select Committee on Intelligence, <u>Hearings.
Part 3. U. S. Intelligence Agencies and Activities: Domestic
Intelligence Programs</u> (Washington: Government Printing Office,
1976), and U. S., Congress, Senate, Select Committee to Study
Governmental Operations with Respect to Intelligence Activi-
ties. <u>Final Report. Book II. Intelligence Activities and
the Rights of Americans</u> (Washington: Government Printing
Office, 1976).

CHAPTER 7

Foreign Problems

Introduction

The foreign problems of the U.S. intelligence community are divided into two categories, reflecting the two basic concerns of American foreign policy in general. One set of problems involves relations with our allies. These are nations with which we share a common heritage, culture, philosophy, and sense of purpose. While other democratic, industrialized nations of the First World are also our allies, the nations of Great Britain and Israel are of special importance in analyzing the foreign intelligence problems of the United States. These problems involve questions of trust, counterintelligence capability, and security. The other set of problems concerns the foreign threats to U.S. intelligence, especially the massive and effective Soviet intelligence apparatus. Soviet policy makers view America as their main adversary and they depend on their secret service to advance Soviet influence abroad and preserve the Soviet system at home.

Allies

Since its inception as the Office of Coordination and Information, U.S. intelligence has maintained a strong liaison with the secret services of its political allies. This relationship began with the wartime necessities of World War II when U.S. and British interests and capabilities were mutually interdependent and in more recent times has been manifested in the close alliance between sections of the U.S. intelligence community and Israeli intelligence. Exchanges of information and occasional joint operations have been routinely conducted with other allies, but the relations with Britain and Israel indicate the range and types of problems inherent in sharing secret information the security of which cannot be guaranteed.

Great Britain. On July 11, 1941, President Roosevelt authorized the creation of the Office of Coordination and Information, the innocuously-titled predecessor to the Office of Strategic Services (OSS). Its director was General William ("Wild Bill") Donovan, an energetic and successful businessman. The major problem facing America's new intelligence organization was that it lacked virtually everything a viable secret agency requires, including experienced headquarters and field personnel, records and record-keeping procedures, and a knowledge of how to build and maintain clandestine capabilities. What it did have, in relative abundance compared to other countries' secret services, was financial and bureaucratic support. The match between OSS needs and resources fit perfectly with British resources and needs.[1]

In the summer of 1941 Britain and Russia were the only countries offering meaningful resistance to German military might. Roosevelt perceived Germany to be a major threat to the future of democracy and thus entered into an "unwritten" alliance with Britain. He anticipated our eventual entry into World War II as a direct military protagonist and foresaw our need for secret information about enemy plans and capabilities. He authorized Donovan to work closely with British intelligence, supplying British needs in return for British expertise and other intelligence prerequisites. The result was a close and friendly personal and professional relationship between Donovan and the head of British intelligence in the Western Hemisphere, William ("Little Bill") Stephenson. Thus, America's intelligence service began with access to an extensive and highly professional intelligence apparatus.

The wartime alliance between the intelligence services of America and Britain was characterized by cooperation between the high-ranking officers but a substantial skepticism at the middle levels. While Donovan and Stephenson, and most of their respective section and department heads, worked in a united effort, many Americans felt the OSS was being used by the British to maintain their empire and prestige and many British resented America's intelligence naivete. This combination of cooperation and conflict continued throughout the war, although generally the conflict was suppressed in the interests of uniting to defeat the common enemy.

Postwar relations between U.S. intelligence, particularly the CIA, and the British Secret Intelligence Service (SIS) have reflected this paradoxical mix of mutual need and mutual suspicion. The historical, cultural, political, and economic relationships between the United States and Great Britain have been generally strong and positive, despite occasional policy disagreements. This has resulted in a continued cooperation in matters of intelligence, including both operations and analyses. However, the history of British intelligence since World War II has been dominated by repeated evidence of penetration by the Soviet intelligence service. The most famous and damaging case involved a Soviet espionage network ("reseau") that operated at the highest levels of British intelligence.[2]

The leader of this Soviet reseau was Harold Adrian Russell ("Kim") Philby. Philby was recruited by Soviet intelligence in the 1930s while a university student. He was impressed with Marxist philosophy and regarded the USSR as the world's best hope and Britain and America as the main obstacles to world socialism. Philby was a brilliant, charming, and sociable individual, who entered public service and eventually rose to the most sensitive post in the British SIS, head of the unit responsible for Soviet counterespionage. In effect, his SIS task was to defend British intelligence from penetration by the Soviets. The results of this astounding breach of security included his ability to alert Moscow to a joint Anglo-American attempt to overthrow the communist regime in Albania in 1951 (an operation with a high probability of success, given that country's geographical accessibility and political vulnerability), and his routine review of espionage reports (including one that threatened to expose him as a Soviet agent, which he neutralized by having Moscow incarcerate the agent before the report was sent).

From 1949 to 1951, Philby was the Washington liaison between the SIS and the CIA and FBI. He worked closely with the CIA's counterespionage head, James Jesus Angleton. While they shared many secrets, both Angleton and Philby had the mutual suspicions which are prerequisite to successful counterespionage work. Angleton was able to penetrate Philby's Washington reseau and while the "doubled" agent could not provide Philby's name, the Angleton-Philby relationship became characterized by an increasing suspicion. Angleton was instrumental in finally alerting London to Philby's true allegiance, but before he could be caught, Philby escaped to Moscow, along with most members of his reseau.

The effects of the Philby episode have been varied and significant. He had knowledge of virtually all major British and many American intelligence secrets, and especially of espionage, counterespionage, and covert actions directed at Eastern Europe and the Soviet Union. His escape in 1963 meant that these operations were necessarily presumed jeopardized. While attempts were made to control the damage, the Philby case has resulted in doubts by American intelligence officers about the wisdom of sharing secrets with the SIS. While there is still a great deal of cooperation between the secret services of the two countries, a lingering reluctance exists, originating in wartime suspicions and jealousy and reinforced by damaging penetrations by the Soviets of British intelligence. This situation presents American intelligence with a crucial problem of reconciling the advantages and necessities of maintaining close relations with our strongest and most important ally with the fear that Britain cannot guarantee the security that such a close relationship requires.

Israel.[3] The factors that characterize Israel's intelligence community are very different from those of U.S. intelligence. The geographic scope of U.S. intelligence needs is global, but Israel's are tightly focused on its region. The U.S. pursues a foreign policy that alternates between cooperation and confrontation with our main adversary (and usually combines both elements in a complex admixture), but Israel maintains a constant and relatively simple policy toward its main antagonists. The U.S. intelligence community's views are sometimes self-contradictory

and are occasionally disregarded by policy makers, but Israeli intelligence is regarded as its first line of defense and is almost
always considered a vital policy-making element. Finally, U.S.
intelligence must operate in an extremely open and diverse society
and against an effectively closed one, but Israel is a unified and
semi-open society operating against closed but porous ones. Despite these differences, cooperation between U.S. and Israeli
intelligence has been close, although the investigations and
revelations of U.S. intelligence activities in the 1970s have
weakened the relationship.

The close relations that existed before the 1970s were a
manifestation of the general relationship between the U.S. and
Israel. Since its founding in 1948, Israel has had a special
relationship with the United States. The U.S. has been Israel's
closest and most dependable ally. This alliance is reflected in
the cooperation between the two respective intelligence communities.

Israeli intelligence is composed of three parts. The intelligence unit of the Foreign Ministry collects diplomatic intelligence
and contributes to intelligence products. The Mossad (Central
Institute for Intelligence and Special Missions) is primarily
responsible for espionage, counterintelligence, and covert actions.
Military Intelligence also engages in clandestine activities, and
it dominates the intelligence production process in Israel. While
there is a degree of the same kinds of bureaucratic competition
that characterize the U.S. intelligence community, Israel's constant state of hostility with its neighbors has meant that the perceptions and analyses of Military Intelligence are usually most
influential.

U.S.-Israeli intelligence relations have been mutually supportive. The U.S. has provided important technical assistance to
the Mossad, including cryptography equipment, and has cooperated
in assisting Israel in covert operations by sharing intelligence
on various targets. Of special importance to Israel is intelligence on Arab, and particularly Palestinian, targets, which U.S.
intelligence has exchanged with Israel since an agreement in 1956.

In that year Nikita Khrushschev, in a celebrated speech to
the 20th Congress of the Communist Party of the Soviet Union, de-
nounced the regime of Joseph Stalin and argued that the Party had
made grievous errors of policy throughout Stalin's long rule.
The CIA, through its own Soviet agents, quickly obtained a summary
of this speech, which had been delivered in secret to the Party
Congress. However, the CIA greatly desired the full text of the
speech, which had profound potential value for policy, propaganda,
and intelligence purposes. The Israeli Mossad obtained a copy of
the speech and gave it to the CIA, together with a pledge that the

Agency could claim credit for obtaining the copy. In return, the Israelis obtained an agreement from DCI Allen Dulles to work closely in intelligence concerns of mutual benefit. Dulles agreed to this bargain, which reinforced the relationship between the two intelligence services. That relationship was greatly influenced by James Jesus Angleton.

Angleton served as the head of the CIA's counterintelligence effort for over two decades. He began his intelligence career working for the OSS in World War II, when he first began working with the Zionist factions that would eventually achieve their goal of a Jewish state and homeland. Angleton supported that goal, and when Israel became a state, he absorbed the Israeli "account," despite the separate existence of a Middle East Division in what was then known as the Clandestine Services unit of the CIA. This part of the CIA was responsible for foreign intelligence collection, counterintelligence and counterespionage, and covert action (e.g., paramilitary operations and propaganda efforts). Clandestine Services, the predecessor to what is now the Directorate of Operations, was divided into geographic divisions, and logically Israel would be the responsibility of the Chief of the Middle East Division. The assignment of Israel to the head of counterespionage was unique and administratively illogical. However, Angleton was to maintain this special jurisdiction over the relationship between U.S. and Israeli intelligence until he left the CIA in 1974. During this period, the Angleton-Israeli connection was cordial and mutually beneficial, and although the general intelligence relationship was somewhat less cordial and beneficial, there was a mutual respect. Events since 1974 have changed this relationship, beginning with Angleton's departure.

The DCI in late 1974 was William Colby who was determined to reveal what he considered the past excesses and improprieties of the U.S. intelligence community. Colby also was complying with the policies of his predecessor, James Schlesinger, to reduce the number of employees in Clandestine Services on the grounds that many of these were "old timers" who had ceased to be productive. Angleton opposed both of these measures, an understandable reaction given his counterintelligence perspective. To reveal any past activities, regardless of their nature, would result in an advantage for the adversarial intelligence services. Also, removing the "old timers" would seriously weaken our counterintelligence capabilities since the arcane world of counterintelligence requires years of experience to adequately understand.

Colby prevailed and Angleton retired, although many argued he was fired.[4] The Israelis, who had come to rely on Angleton as their main benefactor in U.S. intelligence were disappointed and displeased at having to adjust to a new relationship, since with Angleton's departure the Israeli "account" was transferred to the

Middle East Division. Soon after Angleton left the CIA, the 1975 "time of troubles" for the CIA occurred, with its public revelation of past activities and a subsequent rupture of secret and sensitive information regarding intelligence operatives, missions, and methods. The Israelis, like other allied intelligence organizations, became reluctant to maintain close ties with U.S. intelligence, for fear that the secrecy of those ties could not be maintained. A third factor that has lessened the exchange of intelligence between the U.S. and Israel has been the changing posture of the U.S. in its Middle East policy. America no longer automatically and totally supports Israel in that region. While the imperatives of U.S. foreign policy make this shift understandable, Israeli leaders feel that their nation's survival requires a high degree of security and that some skepticism of U.S. motives is necessary.

The KGB[5]

The Committee for State Security (Komitet Gosudarstvennoy Besopasnosti) of the Soviet Union differs considerably from the intelligence community of the United States, although its functions include a similar set of tasks. The difference is based on several factors, including the primary role the KGB plays in Soviet policy making and implementation, the organization and functions of the Soviet intelligence apparatus, and the nature of its targets. The KGB has certain advantages as an intelligence service that its Western, and especially American, counterparts do not have. These advantages derive primarily from four aspects.

Sword and Shield. The crest of the KGB is a sword and a shield, representing the conceptual relationship of the KGB to the Communist Party of the Soviet Union (CPSU). Although nominally an organ of the Soviet government, the KGB is controlled and directed by the CPSU and exists to serve the Party. Its "sword" function is to implement the Party's will throughout the Soviet Union and abroad. In this sense, the KGB is an offensive tool of Soviet policy that serves to transform the domestic and foreign environment of the Party, according to policy choices made by the Politburo, which is the highest level decision-making body in the Soviet Union. The extent to which the KGB is subservient to the Politburo is illustrated by the fact that the Chairman of the KGB (analogous to the American DCI) is a full member of the Politburo. While this appears similar to the DCI's relationship to the National Security Council, it differs because the Politburo makes all significant policy decisions in the Soviet Union and because the DCI's relationship to the NSC depends on his personal relationship with the President while the KGB Chairman is always an important if not critical participant in Politburo deliberations.

The defensive function of the KGB, represented by the shield, is to maintain the Party's position as unchallenged policy maker and implementor. The CPSU dominates political, economic, and social life in the Soviet Union. Soviet government exists to serve the interests of the Party. The KGB's basic "shield" task is to defend the CPSU from its actual and potential enemies and rivals.

The KGB is a tool of the CPSU and as such is subordinate to the Party. Unlike the components of the U.S. intelligence community, the KGB has no separate political base nor does it have any independence. While it may have some degree of operational discretion, it cannot effectively challenge the dictates of the Politburo. Consequently, it is primarily concerned with operations rather than its production of intelligence. It does have the equivalent of the CIA's Directorate of Intelligence, but this is a minor activity in contrast to those Directorates concerned with operations against internal and external protagonists. Thus, its relationship to policy making is quite different from that of the U.S. intelligence community.

Soviet policy makers are frequently far more experienced in the practical aspects of policy making and implementation than American policy makers. Most have prevailed in the struggle to achieve Politburo rank because they are pragmatic politicians. Since they do not have to engage in Western-style electoral politics, their respective images and personalities are insignificant compared to their administrative and policy skills. In a system in which public opinion is virtually meaningless, political success is more a matter of acquiring experience and building support within the Party. This means that those who rise to Politburo status are less inclined to be persuaded by National Intelligence Estimates prepared by the intelligence community. The intelligence products that do flow to the Politburo tend to be more "raw" intelligence than the finished goods produced by the U.S. intelligence community.

Organization. The KGB is a unified structure that controls and directs the intelligence effort of the Soviet Union, especially in the area of operations. While the military has an intelligence branch, the Glavnoye Razvedyvatelnoye Upravleniye (GRU), it operates as a subsidiary of the KGB and despite bureaucratic and policy disputes between KGB and GRU personnel, the KGB dominates the Soviet intelligence apparatus. The combination of both offensive and defensive roles in a single organization that serves the CPSU means that the KGB is a huge structure engaged in a variety of intelligence activities. A U.S. counterpart to the KGB would include the CIA, NSA, most of military intelligence, all of the FBI, and major portions of state and local police and investigatory units. The primary concern of the KGB is protecting the Party from internal threats, including dissidence and border security.

The Soviet Union is composed of a number of different national and ethnic groups. The Party seeks to suppress the desires of these groups for independence and autonomy. It requires the KGB both to defend it against dissident threats to its political preeminence and to attack those who are attempting to foment discontent. This task is an enduring one since the number of groups is large and the potential for political dissidence is high. The geographic and population size of the Soviet Union means that the KGB must devote considerable resources to the surveillance, investigation, penetration, and control of the groups. This monumental task is the responsibility of the KGB's Second and Fifth Chief Directorates, which have no equivalents in the U.S. intelligence community.

The other main domestic concern of the KGB is the jurisdiction of the Border Guards, another Chief Directorate. This body combines police and paramilitary functions to prevent unauthorized passage across the borders of the Soviet Union. A benign analog to the Border Guards would be the U.S. Naturalization and Immigration Service, although the comparison is more conceptual than real. The Border Guards, like the Fifth Chief Directorate, have a herculean task, given the enormous border of the Soviet Union, the frequent restiveness of USSR citizens who live along that border, and the presence of hostile nations whose intelligence organizations seek to penetrate that border. While the problems are less acute on the USSR's western border, border defense against both internal and external sources require significant resources, especially in terms of manpower. Approximately 300,000 individuals are in the Border Guards, more than are employed by the entire U.S. intelligence community.

The First Chief Directorate is the KGB organ that is similar to the CIA's Directorate of Operations. It engages in the same kinds of activities, primarily espionage, counterintelligence and counterespionage, and covert action. It also has Area Departments similar to the Area Divisions of DDO. Unlike the CIA, it contains the smaller version of the CIA's separate Directorate of Science and Technology. It also has units that have no equivalent in the CIA or the U.S. intelligence community, such as the department that controls and coordinates the intelligence services of its allies, especially those in Eastern Europe and Cuba. The KGB, unlike U.S. intelligence, dominates these "little brothers" and, through the First Chief Directorate, uses them in its clandestine activities. The main target of the First Chief Directorate is the U.S. and especially its intelligence apparatus, but China is viewed as another major problem and Western Europe and the Third World are also important considerations.

Two other departments of the First Chief Directorate are of special importance. Department A is responsible for conducting disinformation campaigns, especially against the West. Disinformation is a form of offensive propaganda that includes fabrications, lies, and planted news items that serve to advance Soviet interests by creating a favorable impression of the USSR while simultaneously discrediting Western governments. It seeks to portray the Soviet government as the champion of social progress and military restraint and characterize the West as decadent, elitist, and dangerous to peace. The activities of Department A are aided by the freedom of the press that exists in the West and also by the legitimacy of questioning one's government that characterizes democracy. Operating from within the confines of a closed society, the Soviets are able to control the outflow of news from the USSR. Operating in a free and open society, Western governments must continually justify their actions and policies to an often skeptical electorate. While the CIA and other Western intelligence services also engage in propaganda efforts abroad, the KGB has few of the disadvantages that they have. The effects of the Soviet disinformation campaign have benefitted from the public opinion climate of recent years that is characterized by a critical view of the veracity of government pronouncements (the credibility gap) and a media whose internal competition and external adversarial relationship to government sometimes results in news and analyses whose objectivity is questionable.

Department V is the KGB organ whose task is to eliminate individuals who otherwise cannot be controlled or neutralized. It conducts assassinations and other capital offenses in foreign countries. This is commonly known as the "Department of Wet Affairs" (or "wetwork"), which refers to the occasional bloody consequences of its actions. These actions are rarely directed against the leaders of other countries. Rather, the targets usually are either leaders of groups representing Soviet nationalities who seek support for their activities abroad or certain defectors from the Soviet Union or its allies, especially those who have great value to the intelligence services of Soviet adversaries. In addition to assassinations, Department V is responsible for sabotage of physical structures abroad and is expected to perform these tasks at the direction of the Politburo, especially in time of war.

These are the four Chief Directorates of the KGB. Other less vital, but nonetheless important, parts of the KGB are concerned with administrative responsibilities, providing technical support (analogous to the CIA's Office of Technical Services), communications, and security of buildings and grounds. The KGB is an immense bureaucracy, and suffers from some of the same coordination and control problems that characterize U.S. intelligence although for somewhat different reasons. It is a unified intelligence apparatus under the direction and control of the Party elite, but its sheer size results in a sacrifice of efficiency. Its size also means that it can resist some directives, although such resistance is difficult to maintain over time. Despite these problems, the KGB is a powerful and vital tool of Soviet policy and its power is enhanced by the society in which it operates.

Closed Society. The KGB functions in a closed society. All important decisions, and most minor ones, are made by the CPSU and especially by its elite. The KGB, as the Party's sword and shield, has a unique position in the Soviet Union. It is the primary source of the Party's power since it is the main organ of physical coercion in a society whose political, economic, and social norms are dictated by the Party, operating as the "vanguard of the proletariat." The Party elite argue that the USSR is in a prolonged state of transition from the decadence and fragmentation of the past to the progressive and harmonious future. Because domestic and foreign enemies of the Party are continually trying to defeat its goals, it must exercise complete control over domestic policy and maintain a vigorous posture towards its international adversaries. The Party elite contend that only they know how to pursue the ongoing revolution and that contradictions to their plans to achieve the revolution must be defeated. Only the elite are equipped to rule and opposition must therefore be eliminated ruthlessly. The KGB is the tool of internal suppression and external aggression. In the oligarchic Soviet society, the KGB is the means by which the elite maintain their authority. Consequently, the main task of the KGB is to keep Soviet policy making closed to outsiders. This means that the KGB must be constantly vigilant and responsive to any threats to the Party's dominance over Soviet society.

The assumptions that characterize the democratic industrialized states are not assumed in the Soviet Union. There are no electoral politics and therefore the government is not accountable to its citizens. The Party's control is absolute and institutions such as liberty, meaningful public opinion, independent analyses of and commentaries on official policies and activities, judicial review, and freedoms of speech, press, and assembly are inconsistent with that absolute control and are considered politically heretical. The Party's control must be maintained and the KGB is the main structure that serves that function. Consequently, the only restraints on the KGB are exercised by the Party elite. The KGB is the police in the Soviet police state. Its legal jurisdiction is virtually unchallenged.

This extralegal status in the Soviet society means that membership in the KGB is a valued position. The large size of the KGB inevitably means that not all of its recruits are of high quality. This is especially true of the Border Guards, whose main task requires individuals who are willing to perform relatively menial work. Security requirements are strict, but accommodations must be made to the realities of the job market. So, while the

KGB is an elite organization in Soviet government, some of its elements are not characterized by elite individuals. This means that despite its assigned functions as the sword and shield, it sometimes is inefficient and ineffective. Maintaining absolute control over the Soviet Union is a virtually impossible task given its extremely diverse population, its inability to meet economic productivity requirements, and its often conflicting and contradictory goals and policies. Despite these difficulties, the KGB continues to exercise control and to maintain the Party as the vanguard of the proletariat. The KGB's monumental domestic tasks are matched by its foreign concerns.

Global Scope. The KGB, like the U.S. intelligence community, has a worldwide perspective. Because it is a superpower, the Soviet Union must be concerned with events that occur everywhere. Regardless of whether the USSR is characterized as a defensive or offensive nation in the dynamics of world affairs, its policy makers require an awareness of potential threats and/or opportunities wherever and whenever they arise. In this sense, Soviet and American intelligence are nearly identical since there is no country or region that is unimportant. They are also similar in terms of the priorities they assign to different foreign areas. For each, the other is the prime intelligence target. Since its inception in 1947, the CIA's main concern has been the Soviet Union. Likewise, the KGB has regarded the United States as its main antagonist and has allocated its intelligence resources accordingly. A major difference is the opportunity each has to penetrate the other. Acquiring information and intelligence on any closed society is difficult, but the USSR is an especially challenging task for U.S. intelligence. Conversely, the United States is one of the most open societies and acquisition of information and intelligence is relatively easy for the KGB and its military surrogate, the GRU. U.S. intelligence has partly overcome this imbalance through greater reliance on technical acquisition means, but access to Soviet planning and policy-making intelligence remains a major problem. KGB access to U.S. political, economic, and military planning is often direct since these plans are usually the subjects of open and vigorous public debate. Thus, the open society of America is a much more penetrable intelligence target than the closed society of the Soviet Union. The KGB uses its embassy in Washington, its consulates in New York, Chicago, and San Francisco, its United Nations delegation, and its official and semi-official trade missions and businesses as covers for intelligence operatives. While U.S. intelligence surely uses U.S. representatives in the USSR as cover, the Soviets have more intelligence personnel in America since they tend to rely more on HUMINT than U.S. intelligence does and because they have the added advantage of using the Soviet and allied missions to the United Nations in New York as covers. KGB activities in the U.S. are extensive and eclectic, covering military, political, economic, and particularly in recent years, technological aspects of America's prospects, potentials, and policies.

The United States is the primary focus of the KGB's First Chief Directorate, which is concerned with foreign intelligence and espionage. Other departments of this Directorate include Western Europe, Latin America, Asia, Africa, and the Middle East. The KGB not only seeks to know what is happening in these areas, but also to influence events. In attempting to export its doctrine and dominance, the different types of countries demand different strategies. In the open, democratic, pluralistic societies of Western Europe plus Australia, New Zealand, and Japan, the disinformation efforts of Department A are emphasized. In the often turbulent countries of the Third World, where there are various sources of discontent with the status quo, more direct means of covert action are frequently used, especially support for "wars of national liberation." Unlike the United States, endorsement by Soviet policy makers for foreign involvement is not the subject of public debate, and even within the Politburo disagreements tend to revolve around pragmatic concerns rather than questions of the legitimacy or propriety of trying to influence or direct events in other countries.

Conclusion

The foreign environment of the U.S. intelligence community presents several major problems. Relations with allied governments and their respective intelligence services are never completely cordial and sometimes are characterized by doubt and distrust. High-level KGB penetration of the intelligence organizations of our most important allies have resulted in a reluctance by the CIA and other U.S. intelligence organizations to share important data that is crucial to an allied intelligence effort. Public disclosures by U.S. institutions, especially the Congress and the media, of clandestine activities conducted by our intelligence apparatus have made our allies less willing to cooperate with us. While cooperation does exist, the various intelligence communities of the democratic, industrialized nations maintain a mutual skepticism of each other's security and confidentiality. The degree of cooperation and common purpose is more confederal than unitary.

The main foreign antagonist of U.S. intelligence is the Soviet KGB. It has the advantage of operating in and for an elite, closed society. Its position in that society is unchallenged and unchallengeable. It retains the confidence of the ruling elite and is indispensable to that elite. As the sword and the shield of the Party, it is both the offensive and defensive tool used to advance external influence and internal authority. It is a unified intelligence organ, although its size and functional diversity preclude maximum efficiency or effectiveness. It has global interests, but its first priority is to challenge the United States and to penetrate American society, including its intelligence establishment.

Faced with these external problems, together with the internal dilemmas and domestic situations discussed in Chapters 5 and 6, the U.S. intelligence community is at a decisive period in its history and development. Policy makers continue to require its products in order to base their decisions on accurate, viable, and plausible assessments. Those policy makers also continue to require appropriate tools of foreign policy to sufficiently implement those decisions. To remain a strong and effective country, the United States requires a strong and effective intelligence community. In order to be strong and effective, the internal, domestic, and foreign problems of the U.S. intelligence community must be resolved. In the changing environments, the problems continue to grow. The basic problem for the U.S. intelligence community is whether the environmental problems can be resolved before they become insoluble.

NOTES

1. Thomas F. Troy, Donovan and the CIA: A History of the Estab-
    lishment of the Central Intelligence Agency (Washington:
    Central Intelligence Agency, 1981), William Stevenson, A Man
    Called Intrepid: The Secret War (New York: Harcourt, Brace,
    Javanovich, 1976), Anthony Cave Brown, War Report of the OSS
    (New York: Berkley Madallion Books, 1976), and R. Harris
    Smith, OSS: The Secret History of America's First Central
    Intelligence Agency (Berkeley, CA: University of California
    Press, 1972).

2. Harold Adrian Russell ("Kim") Philby, My Silent War (New York:
    Grove Press, 1968), Bruce Page with David Leitch and Philip
    Knightley, The Philby Conspiracy (Garden City, NY: Doubleday,
    1968), and Andrew Boyle, The Fourth Man: The Definitive
    Account of Kim Philby, Guy Burgess and Donald MacLean and Who
    Recruited Them to Spy for Russia (New York: Dial Press, 1979).

3. Michael Bar-Zohar, Spies in the Promised Land: Iser Harel
    and the Israeli Secret Service (Boston: Houghton Mifflin,
    1972), Mohammed Heikal, The Road to Ramadan (New York: Quad-
    rangle Books, 1975), and Chaim Herzog, The War of Atonement:
    October 1973 (Boston: Little, Brown and Company, 1975).

4. William E. Colby, Honorable Men: My Life in the CIA (New
    York: Simon and Schuster, 1978) and Cord Meyer, Facing Real-
    ity: From World Federalism to the CIA (New York: Harper and
    Row, 1980).

5. John Barron, KGB: The Secret Work of Soviet Secret Agents
    (New York: Reader's Digest Press, 1974), David J. Dallin,
    Soviet Espionage (New Haven, CT: Yale University Press,
    1955), Peter Deriabin and Frank Gibney, The Secret World
    (Garden City, NY: Doubleday, 1959), Aleksi Myagkov, Inside
    the KGB: An Expose by an Officer of the Third Directorate
    (New Rochelle, NY: Arlington House, 1977), Vladimir Sakharov
    and Umberto Tosi, High Treason (New York: G. P. Putman's
    Sons, 1980), and Rupert Sigl, In the Claws of the KGB:
    Memoirs of a Double Agent (Ardmore, PA: Dorrance and Company,
    1978).

APPENDIX

The Organization and Operation of a Reseau[1]

Introduction

U.S. intelligence professionals use the French word reseau to refer to what is commonly known as a "spy network." While every reseau has unique features, depending on its geographical location, its targets, and its personnel, certain principles of espionage are reflected in the organization and operation of any reseau. The popular notion of a "spy" or espionage agent connotes an individual operating alone under the direct control of the head of the nation's secret service. This agent, who usually has a "license to kill," normally ignores any bureaucracy as inconvenient and relies on wits and serendipity to accomplish his or her task, which almost invariably serves to save mankind from some form of disaster. The real world of espionage bears little resemblance to this fictionalized world of spies and counterspies. Most agents operate according to established patterns and under rigid control. In order to understand how information is collected by human sources (HUMINT), it is important to know how a reseau is organized and what principles guide its operation.

Organization

An ideal reseau reflects two fundamental characteristics, chain of command and compartmentation. The term chain of command means that each person in the organization receives his or her directions from a single source and, in turn, is the source for the directions given to the next person in the chain. In this way, the general needs of the individuals at the top of the chain (e.g., the President or the DCI) gain greater specificity and definition as those needs are converted into actions by the time the message is transmitted to the bottom of the chain. The chain of command principle results in control and responsibility. In issuing a "command" to a subordinate, a superior can control the actions of that subordinate by monitoring, auditing, and adjusting those actions according to the situation. This principle is common to all bureaucratic entities, but is especially relevant to intelligence work with its dynamic activities.

The principle of compartmentation is less common among other bureaucracies, but is fundamental to a successful reseau. Compartmentation means organizing and operating a reseau so that its relationships to other, allied organizations cannot be determined. If compartmentation is achieved, exposure of the existence of a reseau or even part of a reseau will not result in knowledge of that reseau's source of control. Basically, compartmentation is designed to thwart the efforts of the target's counterespionage apparatus. Effective compartmentation means that if the target

103

discovers hostile espionage activity, it will be unable to adequately discern the extent or intent of that activity. The idea of compartmentation is summarized in the phrase "need to know." Only those individuals in the organization who "need to know" something (e.g., a policy posture, an agent's true identity, or an espionage mission) are allowed to know it.

Chain of command and compartmentation are reflected in the organization of a "typical" CIA reseau, shown in the chart on the next page. The key individual is the Case Officer, who serves as the link between the reseau and the rest of the intelligence organization. The roles of the President, the NSC, the DCI, and the DDO are discussed in Chapters 3 and 4. The three staffs of the Directorate of Operations, Foreign Intelligence (FI), Counterintelligence (CI), and Covert Action (CA), assist the DDO in task assignments and definitions and provide direction and functional support for the various CIA stations.

The world is divided by the Directorate of Operations into a number of stations. Each station has clearly defined geographic boundaries, and virtually all CIA clandestine activity that occurs in any one station is subject to the control of the Chief of Station (COS). Normally, the boundaries of a station will coincide with the boundaries of a country. However, in the case of a large country or one that is otherwise inconsistent with management from a single station, a country may be divided into two or more stations. The Soviet Union is the most obvious example, since its huge geographic size, unrivaled political and strategic importance, and admittedly effective counterespionage capabilities require an extensive clandestine effort. Conversely, a small, friendly country might be combined with its neighbor into a single station for reasons of economy. Thus, while the norm is one station per country, the number of CIA stations is not equal to the number of countries in the world at any one time.

Typically, each Chief of Station is responsible for all clandestine activities conducted in that station. The COS has a staff to assist in the areas of FI, CI, and where relevant, CA. However, these staffs normally are quite small and frequently the COS must reflect expertise in all facets of clandestine operations. The COS almost always operates under embassy cover and is ostensibly part of the official diplomatic community. This entitles the COS to diplomatic immunity, which means that he or she is not subject to arrest, detention, trial, or incarceration. Should the COS be so amateurish as to make his or her actions obvious or obnoxious to the host country, the result may be diplomatic expulsion as a persona non grata. Other station employees who serve under diplomatic cover are also protected under the customs and treaties of international law.

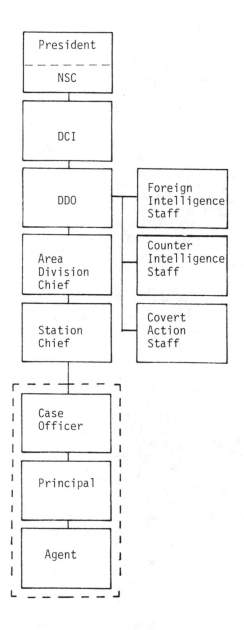

A <u>Reseau</u>: Components and Chain of Command

Another advantage of diplomatic cover is the high visibility it provides for station personnel in the local community. The U.S. government encourages its overseas personnel to become active in community life abroad as a way of "personalizing" U.S. foreign policy. Station personnel who belong to social and athletic clubs and who talk to fraternal, business, and civic organizations are simultaneously able to maintain their covers and establish the contacts that are a prerequisite to successful clandestine activity.

There are two major disadvantages to diplomatic cover, despite its legal protection and intelligence accessibility. Official cover implies official duties, and those duties must be performed or the cover is "blown." Station personnel who operate out of embassies, consulates, and other U.S. offices abroad must work at two jobs, the official one and the clandestine one. This results in long hours and a great psychological strain. Understandably, intelligence personnel who serve overseas for extended periods of time suffer high rates of divorce, alcoholism, and other aspects of emotional and mental stress. In addition to these personal problems, dividing one's efforts between official and clandestine duties means that the clandestine work can never be fully pursued. This problem can be solved by adding additional intelligence personnel to the station, although this solution may not be feasible because of budgetary or political limits on the size of the official delegation.

The other main disadvantage in official cover is the stress it generates on the U.S. diplomatic community in the station area. There is usually friction between intelligence personnel and the "legitimate" representatives of the U.S. government. State Department employees in particular tend to view their mission abroad quite differently from CIA employees, and often the Foreign Service Officer (FSO) will feel that CIA activities or even presence in a country are counterproductive to U.S. foreign policy objectives. The FSO and the station employee often are mutually suspicious and each tends to regard the work of the other as a frustration or obstacle to fulfilling his or her mission. While the Ambassador is officially and ostensibly the Station Chief's superior, the COS often is more knowledgeable about the country and sometimes is viewed as more reliable and dependable by the local regime. Thus, there is a mutual resentment between the diplomats and the clandestine officers, although in most cases the debilitating effects of this attitude are ameliorated to some extent by the personal relationship between the Ambassador and the COS.

In addition to the COS and the station staff personnel, most Case Officers will have official cover. The Case Officer is the main connection between the Chief of Station, who receives directives from headquarters, and the agents, who acquire the informa-

tion the directives request. The number of Case Officers assigned
to a station depends on a number of factors, including the importance of the station, the permeability of the target country, and
the number of covers the official delegation can justify. Each
Case Officer (CO) is responsible for recruiting agents who will be
assigned espionage tasks. Only in the most unusual circumstances
will an American become an espionage "agent." Thus, the CO is
the lowest-ranking American in a typical intelligence apparatus,
although he or she is the highest-ranking individual in a reseau.
The successful operation of a reseau depends on the training,
skills, and experience of the Case Officer. Case Officers are
sent through a number of "schools" by the CIA. These schools, run
by the Directorate of Administration's Office of Training, emphasize the techniques of espionage that are necessary to the effective management of a reseau.

The principle of compartmentation greatly influences the
organization of a reseau. While Case Officers usually are aware
of much of the station's intelligence mission as a result of
periodic conferences chaired by the COS, the individuals who work
for a single Case Officer are subject to the "need to know" axiom.
This means that the reseau should be designed to insure secrecy
and security. Case Officers try to achieve this goal by insula-
ting the members of the reseau from each other. While this
results in some extremely complex arrangements, nearly every
reseau has two participants in addition to the Case Officer,
the Principal Agent and the Agent.

Principal. The Principal (Agent) serves as a link between the
Case Officer and the actual espionage agent. Frequently the Case
Officer-Principal relationship is strong and often it is a personal
as well as professional one. The main role of the Principal is to
help the CO to operate the reseau. Usually the Principal is a
native of the country in which the station is located and has
access to one or more groups in that society. Case Officers are
especially interested in working with Principals with access to
the social, economic, and political elite of the country since
that group has the greatest impact on policy.

If the task of the reseau is to acquire foreign intelligence,
the emphasis will be on collection of information, especially
policy-making deliberations. If the station can learn in advance
of changes in policy, this information can be extremely useful in
making and implementing appropriate U.S. policies. If the task
of the reseau is to engage in covert action, the emphasis will be
on influencing events in the target country. This may include
propaganda activities, political, social, or economic operations,
or, in rare cases, paramilitary ventures. While there is a general
intelligence mission for each station, the variety of specific
tasks means that a number of different kinds of reseaux are

necessary. Consequently, each Case Officer needs several Principals, unknown to each other in the interests of security and compartmentation, in order to maximize his or her access to appropriate agents. Case Officers spend considerable time in cultivating
relationships with actual and potential Principals since they serve
as the connection to the agent.

Agent. This is the lowest-ranking individual in a reseau. An
agent normally is recruited and controlled by a Case Officer,
via a Principal. Occasionally a station will receive a "walk-in,"
an agent who volunteers to conduct espionage for the United States.
Walk-ins are treated with great skepticism, since they may be
seeking to penetrate U.S. intelligence as a counterespionage agent
for a rival secret service. While walk-ins are never fully
accredited by the Counterintelligence Staff of a station, they
may contribute significant intelligence if they are genuine. One
of the best examples of a walk-in was the Soviet Colonel Oleg
Penkovsky who relayed Top Secret material on Soviet strategic
military capabilities to Western intelligence for several years
before he was discovered, tried, and executed by Soviet counterespionage.

Walk-ins require little cultivation since they actively
volunteer their services. Conversely, the recruitment and handling
of agents is often a slow, laborious, and sometimes tedious exercise which is not always successful. It requires careful planning
by the Case Officer, who must employ skills, techniques, and
expertise from a variety of fields. It is the Case Officer who
must determine how to "run" the Agent and operate the reseau.

Operation

A Case Officer constructs a reseau and staffs it with the
appropriate individuals (the Principal, the Agent, and other
personnel) to accomplish some defined task. This task is determined by the chain of command, but usually the task is general
and durable. Construction of an ad hoc reseau is very rare since
it usually takes a long time and a great deal of patience to
establish the connections between the Case Officer and the Agent.
The definition of the task assigned to the reseau normally follows
a four-stage pattern. Initially, some target is specified. For
most stations, the primary target is the Soviet embassy, including
its KGB apparatus. Other common targets for long-term penetration
and influence include the nation's Communist Party, trade unions,
the local media, influential politicians, and other social, economic, and political groups in the country that are salient or potentially salient. Targets are specified either because of their
basic interest to U.S. foreign policy or because of their particular importance in a specific region or country.

Once a target has been specified, a plan is designed. A major consideration at this stage is whether clandestine activity is required. In many cases, the target may be approachable by and amenable to overt methods such as traditional diplomacy. However, if the plan is designed by the station, it usually includes clandestine activities, even if overt methods may be more appropriate. The plan includes determining the proper mix of espionage, counterespionage, and covert action. Most targets involve basic espionage conducted by agents who attempt to obtain information under the control and direction of the Case Officer. Also, care must be taken to keep the agents' activities secret, so counterespionage is always a factor in the planning stage. Finally, covert action may be appropriate or necessary, depending on the target and the task.

The third stage of task definition is to acquire the necessary support to implement the plan. This involves physical items, including money and any relevant "tools," such as cameras, recording devices, printing presses, or even military hardware. Support also takes the form of endorsement of the plan by higher-ranking members of the chain of command. This bureaucratic and political support is often crucial when the plan is designed for long-term implementation requiring continuity and consistency of policy regarding the importance of the target.

The final phase is the operation of the plan, or its implementation. The focus of this stage is the reseau, and its success is largely a function of the expertise and professionalism of the Case Officer and the relationship between the Case Officer and the Agent. The Case Officer is responsible for establishing and maintaining this relationship and is guided by certain principles of "tradecraft." The foundations of these principles are patience and persistence, and a successful Case Officer manifests the skills of educator, psychologist, administrator, and guidance counselor.

A fundamental principle for the successful operation of a reseau is control. The Case Officer must be in control of the reseau and its personnel throughout the operation. The Principal, the Agent, and other members of the group must be responsive to the directions and orders of the Case Officer and must not engage in activities that threaten the success of the operation. Establishing absolute and authoritative control over a reseau depends on finding the proper inducement for the prospective Agent. The Case Officer discusses the plan with an appropriate Principal, employing the necessary compartmentation limits. Together they review potential Agents according to several fundamental criteria.

The most important criterion is accessibility to the target. Obviously, it does no good to recruit an Agent who cannot contribute to the operation. If the target is the Soviet embassy, the best Agent would be someone with high diplomatic rank or with continual access to embassy communications. However, these people are extremely difficult to recruit since they are usually intensely loyal or they are the subject of intense scrutiny by the KGB counterespionage efforts. Thus, it is often not possible to recruit an Agent with direct and immediate access to the target. Normally, an Agent will be recruited who has potential access, and it is in these cases that the expertise of the Case Officer becomes critical in controlling, managing, and directing the progress of the Agent toward target access. The key factor in this kind of continuing operation is the motivations of the Agent.

What makes a person willing to engage in espionage? The answers are numerous and varied in their combinations. Money is the prime inducement, as are sex, drugs, and other physical inducements. Some people "spy" because they are ideologically committed to a certain cause. Threat of exposure and ridicule make blackmail a useful method of recruiting and controlling an Agent. Another reason individuals become Agents is the subjective excitement of doing something secret and, to the Agent, important, a status factor. The Case Officer and the Principal will decide which of these factors are most likely to succeed and will reduce the list of potential Agents by combining considerations of accessibility, appropriate inducements, and other items such as emotional stability, family responsibilities, the probability of a durable relationship, and the consequences for the operation should the Agent fail to respond to the Case Officer's continuing control.

Following the decision to focus on a particular individual, the Case Officer and the Principal determine the recruitment pattern. Because the Case Officer is concerned with compartmentation and is often unable to approach the prospective Agent because they share little in common, the Principal usually acts as the recruiter. The initial contact, the offer of the inducements, and the gestation period of the Principal-Agent relationship require constant supervision and adjustments by the Case Officer. Because the factors of reseau operation are numerous and varied, there is no one standard way to recruit, train, and control an Agent. The general guidelines for Case Officers include establishing the dependence of the Agent on the rewards of the reseau and making certain that the Agent reports accurately and truthfully to the reseau. An Agent who does not have to rely on the physical, emotional, or ideological benefits of the reseau will not consistently respond to directives. Also, an Agent who feels the need to fabricate or distort information is not very useful to the operation of the reseau.

The work of a Case Officer is extremely complicated. Normally, a Case Officer will be responsible for several operations at

110

the same time. These may be in different stages, and each involves a unique set of factors. He or she must exercise control of each reseau, but be sensitive to the needs of the members of that group. The Case Officer also must work at the "cover" job. Because clandestine operations often are designed for continuing penetration of targets, Case Officers frequently remain at a station for extended periods of time, and most stations are in the less attractive foreign duty posts. (Extending a Case Officer's tour of duty beyond the normal two years of the Foreign Service Officer's tour causes credibility problems and tours of duty are closely monitored by intelligence services attempting to identify CIA employees who are operating under diplomatic cover.) The success and ultimate value of the station depends on the ability of its Case Officers to meet these challenges and effectively organize and control the station's clandestine activities.

Conclusion

The main contribution of a typical reseau is HUMINT. While occasionally a reseau will be constructed strictly for acquisition of technological intelligence, the basic purpose of a reseau is to obtain information on the activities, plans, and policy deliberations of individuals or groups who are trying to maintain security. The reseau is designed and operated to penetrate that security, to spy on the targeted individual or group. The organization and operation of the reseau combines CIA control of its activities with plausible deniability for the actual espionage activity. Espionage does involve the danger and excitement popularized in spy novels. But in real life it also is characterized by careful thinking, great patience, and continued persistence.

NOTES

1. Paul W. Blackstock, The Strategy of Subversion: Manipulating the Politics of Other Nations (Chicago: Quadrangle Books, 1964), Christopher Felix, A Short Course in the Secret War (New York: Dutton, 1963), Sanche de Gramont, The Secret War: The Story of International Espionage Since World War II (New York: G. P. Putnam's Sons, 1962), Victor L. Marchetti and John D. Marks, The CIA and the Cult of Intelligence (New York: Alfred A. Knopf, 1974), Miles Copeland, Without Cloak or Dagger: The Truth About the New Espionage (New York: Simon and Schuster, 1974), Harry Rositzke, The CIA's Secret Operations: Espionage, Counterespionage, and Covert Action (New York: Reader's Digest Press, 1977), Philip Agee, Inside the Company: CIA Diary (New York: Stonehill, 1975), Roy Godson, ed., Intelligence Requirements for the 1980's: Counterintelligence (1980), Covert Action (1981), and Clandestine Collection (1982) (Washington: National Strategy Information Center, Inc.), and David Atlee Phillips, The Night Watch: 25 Years of Peculiar Service (New York: Antheneum, 1977).

BIBLIOGRAPHY

Introduction

The literature on intelligence is extensive. It includes biographies and autobiographies, edited collections of "spy" stories (real and fictional), works that are critical of the intelligence community in part or as a whole, other works that support the community in part or as a whole, government publications, and the vast number of novels on "intelligence." Also, few works can be conveniently classified into any one category. For instance, there are a number of autobiographies and biographies that include frequent observations on various problems of the intelligence community as well as proposed solutions. Finally, the topic of intelligence has an inherent subjectivity in terms of its description and evaluation. The author's perspective is critical to the work's conclusions. These factors result in great variation regarding authenticity, bias, focus, and intent. The classification of this bibliography uses the <u>primary</u> objective of each work, realizing that most entries can be listed under several categories.

Autobiographies and Biographies

These books are about intelligence officers of the United States in the post-World War II period. In relating these stories, authors invariably indicate problems of the intelligence community, but they all use a biographical approach.

Agee, Philip. <u>Inside the Company: Cia Diary</u>. New York: Stonehill Publishing Co., 1975.

Cline, Ray S. <u>Secrets, Spies and Scholars: Blueprint of the Essential CIA</u>. Washington: Acropolis Books, Ltd., 1976.

Colby, William E. <u>Honorable Men: My Life in the CIA</u>. New York: Simon and Schuster, 1978.

De Silva, Peer. <u>Sub Rosa: The CIA and the Uses of Intelligence</u>. New York: New York Times Book Co., 1978.

Ford, Corey. <u>Donovan of OSS</u>. Boston: Little, Brown and Co., 1970.

Kirkpatrick, Lyman B., Jr. <u>The Real CIA</u>. New York: Macmillan Company, 1978.

Meyer, Cord. <u>Facing Reality: From World Federalism to the CIA</u>. New York: Harper and Row, 1980. (paperback edition published by University Press of America in 1982).

Mosley, Leonard. Dulles: A Biography of Eleanor, Allen, and John Foster Dulles and Their Family Network. New York: Dial Press, 1978.

Phillips, David Atlee. The Night Watch: 25 Years of Peculiar Service. New York: Atheneum, 1977.

Powers, Thomas. The Man Who Kept the Secrets: Richard Helms & the CIA. New York: Alfred A. Knopf, 1979.

Troy, Thomas F. Donovan and the CIA: A History of the Establishment of the Central Intelligence Agency. Washington: Central Intelligence Agency, 1981.

Van Der Rhoer, Edward. Deadly Magic: A Personal Account of Communications Intelligence in World War II in the Pacific. New York: Charles Scribner's Sons, 1978.

Walters, Vernon A. Silent Missions. New York: Doubleday & Co., 1978.

OSS and World War II

These books deal primarily with the history, structures, functions, and operations of the Office of Strategic Services and other World War II intelligence agencies and activities of the United States.

Alsop, Stewart and Braden, Thomas. Sub Rosa: The OSS and American Espionage. New York: Harcourt, Brace & World, Inc., 1964.

Farago, Ladislas. The Broken Seal: The Story of "Operation MAGIC" and the Pearl Harbor Disaster. New York: Random House, 1967.

Holmes, Wilfred J. Double-Edged Secrets: U.S. Naval Intelligence Operations in the Pacific during World War II. New York: Farrar, Straus and Co., 1963.

Ind, Allison. Allied Intelligence Bureau: Our Secret Weapon in the War Against Japan. New York: McKay, 1958.

Patti, Archimedes L. A. Why Vietnam: Prelude to America's Albatross. Berkeley: University of California Press, 1980.

Persico, Joseph E. Piercing the Reich: The Penetration of Nazi Germany by American Secret Agents during World War II. New York: Viking Press, 1979.

Smith, R. Harris, OSS: The Secret History of America's First
    Central Intelligence Agency. Berkeley: University of Cali-
    fornia Press, 1972.

U.S. War Department. War Report of the OSS (Office of Stregetic
    Services). New York: Walker and Company, 1976.

Case Studies

These works include descriptive as well as analytical approaches. Some reveal aspects of the "tradecraft" of clandestine
service (espionage, counterespionage, and covert action).

Bernikow, Louise, Abel. New York: Trident Press, 1970.

Blackstock, Paul W. The Strategy of Subversion: Manipulating the
    Politics of Other Nations. Chicago: Quadrangle Books, 1964.

Boveri, Margaret. Treason in the Twentieth Century. New York:
    G.P. Putnam, 1963.

Copeland, Miles. Without Cloak or Dagger: The Truth about the
    New Espionage. New York: Simon and Schuster, 1974.

Cruickshank, Charles G. Deception in World War II. New York:
    Oxford University Press, 1979.

Dulles, Allen W. The Craft of Intelligence. New York: Harper &
    Row, 1963.

Gramont, Sanche de. The Secret War: The Story of International
    Espionage Since World War II. New York: G.P. Putnam, 1962.

Kahn, David. The Codebreakers: The Story of Secret Writing.
    New York: Macmillan, 1967.

Kirkpatrick, Lyman B., Jr. The U.S. Intelligence Community:
    Foreign Policy and Domestic Activities. New York: Hill and
    Wang, 1973.

Klass, Phillip J. Secret Sentries in Space. New York: Random
    House, 1971.

Roosevelt, Kermit. Countercoup: The Struggle for the Control of
    Iran. New York: McGraw-Hill Book Co., 1979.

Rositzke, Harry. The CIA's Secret Operations: Espionage, Counter-
    espionage, and Covert Action. New York: Reader's Digest
    Press, 1977.

Shackley, Theodore. The Third Option: An American View of Counter-insurgency Operations. New York: McGraw-Hill Book Co., 1981.

Sun Tzu. The Art of War. New York: Oxford University Press, 1963.

Taylor, John W. R. and Monday, David. Spies in the Sky. New York: Charles Scribner's Sons, 1972.

Analytical

The basic purpose of these entries is to analyze various aspects and problems of the intelligence community. They attempt to be objective and focus on practical solutions.

Blum, Richard H., ed. Surveillance and Espionage in a Free Society: A Report by the Planning Group on Intelligence and Security to the Policy Council of the Democratic National Committee. New York: Praeger, 1972.

Clark, Keith C. and Legere, Lawrence J., eds. The President and the Management of National Security: A Report by the Institute for Defense Analyses. New York: Praeger, 1969.

Freedman, Lawrence. U. S. Intelligence and the Soviet Strategic Threat. Boulder, Colorado: Westview Press, 1977.

Godson, Roy, ed. Intelligence Requirements for the 1980's. Washington: National Strategy Information Center, Inc.

Volume One: Elements Of Intelligence, 1979.

Volume Two: Analysis and Estimates, 1980.

Volume Three: Counterintelligence, 1980

Volume Four: Covert Action, 1981.

Volume Five: Clandestine Collection, 1982.

Heuer, Richards J., Jr., ed. Quantitative Approaches to Political Intelligence: The CIA Experience. Boulder, Colorado: Westview Press, 1978.

Kent, Sherman. Strategic Intelligence for American World Policy. Princeton, New Jersey: Princeton University Press, 1949.

Knorr, Klaus. Foreign Intelligence and the Social Sciences. Princeton, New Jersey: Princeton University Press, 1964.

116

Pfaltzgraff, Robert L., et al, eds. Intelligence Policy and National Security. Hamden, Connecticut: Shoestring Press, Inc., 1981.

Ransom, Harry Howe. The Intelligence Establishment. Cambridge, Massachusetts: Harvard University Press, 1970.

Wilensky, Harold L. Organizational Intelligence: Knowledge and Policy in Government & Industry. New York: Basic Books, 1967.

Wohlstetter, Roberta. Cuba and Pearl Harbor: Hindsight and Foresight. Santa Monica, California: Rand Corporation, 1965.

_____. Pearl Harbor: Warning and Decision. Stanford: Stanford University Press, 1962.

Critical

Like the analytical works, these books deal with the problems of the intelligence community. Unlike the analytical works, they involve greater subjectivity and emphasize the ineptitude and impropriety of intelligence community activities. Some of them question the necessity of maintaining a U. S. intelligence capability, and a few of them are intended to eliminate any U. S. intelligence capability.

Agee, Philip and Wolf, Louis, eds. Dirty Work: The CIA in Western Europe. Seacaucus, New Jersey: Lyle Stuart, Inc., 1978.

Berman, Jerry J. and Halparin, Morton H. The Abuses of the Intelligence Agencies. Washington: Center for National Security Studies, 1975.

Borosage, Robert L. and Marks, John, eds. The CIA File. New York: Grossman Publishers, 1976.

Corson, William R. The Armies of Ignorance: The Rise of the American Intelligence Empire. New York: The Dial Press, 1977.

McGarvey, Patrick J. CIA: The Myth and the Madness. New York: Saturday Review Press, 1972.

Ray, Ellen, et al, eds. Dirty Work II: The CIA in Africa. Seacaucus, New Jersey: Lyle Stuart, Inc., 1979.

117

Snepp, Frank. Decent Interval: An Insider's Account of Saigon's Indecent End. New York: Random House, 1977.

Stockwell, John. In Search of Enemies: A CIA Story. New York: W. W. North & Co., 1978.

Wise, David and Ross, Thomas B. The Invisible Government. New York: Random House, 1964.

Wyden, Peter. Bay of Pigs: The Untold Story. New York: Simon and Schuster, 1979.

Other Countries

Some of these works are not contemporary, but are included because they illustrate various approaches to the intelligence profession. They are grouped according to the country that bene- fitted from the intelligence organization or operation. Thus, while Harold Adrian Russell ("Kim") Philby eventually became the head of British counterespionage, he remained a KGB agent, and books about Philby are listed under the U.S.S.R. heading.

General

Grammont, Sanche de. The Secret War: The Story of International Espionage Since World War II. New York: G. P. Putnam's Sons, 1962.

Wise, David and Ross, Thomas B. The Espionage Establishment. New York: Random House, 1967.

Australia

Australia, Commonwealth of. Report of the Royal Commission on Es- pionage. Sydney: A. H. Pettifer, 1955.

_____. Report of the Royal Commission on Intelligence and Security. Canberra: Australian Government Publishing Ser- vice, 1977.

Canada

Canada. Commission of Inquiry Concerning Certain Activities of the Royal Canadian Mounted Police. Security and Information. First Report. Hull, Quebec, Canada: Canadian Government Publishing Centre, October 9, 1979.

118

_____. The Report of the Royal Commission to Investigate the Facts Relating to and the Circumstances Surrounding the Communication, by Public Officials and Other Persons in Positions of Trust, of Secret and Confidential Information to Agents of a Foreign Power. Ottawa: Cloutier, 1946.

_____. Royal Commission on Security. Report of the Royal Commission on Security (Abridged). Ottawa: The Queen's Printer, 1969.

China

Deacon, Richard. The Chinese Secret Service. New York: Ballantine Books, 1974.

Czechoslovokia

Bittman, Ladislav. The Deception Game: Czechoslovak Intelligence in Soviet Political Warfare. Syracuse, NY: Syracuse Research Corporation, 1972.

Cuba

Castro-Hidalgo, Orlando. Spy for Fidel. Miami: E. A. Seeman Publisher, 1974.

France

Vosjoli, Philippe L. Thyraud de. Lamia. Boston: Little, Brown and Company, 1970.

Germany

Brissaud, Andre. Canaris: A Biography of Admiral Canaris, Chief of German Military Intelligence in the Second World War. New York: Grosset and Dunlap, 1974.

_____. The Nazi Secret Service. New York: W. W. Norton & Company, 1974.

Gehlen, Reinhard. The Service: The Memoirs of General Reinhard Gehlen. New York: World Publishing, 1972.

Hagen, Louis E. The Secret War for Europe: A Dossier of Espionage. New York: Stein and Day, 1969.

119

Leverkeuhn, Paul. German Military Intelligence. New York: Praeger, 1954.

Great Britain

Beesly, Patrick. Very Special Intelligence: The Story of the Admiralty's Operational Intelligence Centre, 1939-1945. Garden City, N.Y.: Doubleday, 1978.

Calvocoressi, Peter. Top Secret Ultra. New York: Pantheon Books, 1980.

Foot, Michael Richard Daniel. SOE in France: An Account of the Work of the British Special Operations Executive in France, 1940-1944. London: Her Majesty's Stationery Office, 1966.

Hinsley, Francis H., et al. British Intelligence in the Second World War: Its Influence on Strategy and Operations. New York: Cambridge University Press, 1979.

Lewin, Ronald. Ultra Goes to War. New York: McGraw-Hill Book Company, 1978.

Masterman, Sir John C. The Double-Cross System in the War of 1939 to 1945. New Haven, CT: Yale University Press, 1972.

Montagu, Ewen E. S. Beyond Top Secret Ultra. New York: Coward, McCann & Geoghegan, 1978.

Popov, Dusko. Spy/Counterspy: The Autobiography of Dusko Popov. New York: Grosset and Dunlap, 1974.

_____. The Man Who Never Was. Revised edition. Philadelphia: J. B. Lippincott, 1967.

Stevenson, William. A Man Called Intrepid: The Secret War. New York: Harcourt, Brace and Javanovich, 1976.

Israel

Bar-Zohar, Michael. Spies in the Promised Land: Iser Harel and the Israeli Secret Service. Boston: Houghton Mifflin, 1972.

El-Ad, Avri with James Creech III. Decline of Honor. Chicago: Henry Regnery Company, 1976.

Herzog, Chaim. The War of Atonement: October 1973. Boston: Little, Brown and Company, 1975.

Lotz, Wolfgang. The Champagne Spy: Israel's Master Spy Tells His Story. New York: St. Martin's Press, 1972.

Japan

Seth, Ronald. Secret Servants: A History of Japanese Espionage. New York: Farrar, Straus and Cudahy, 1957.

Poland

Monat, Pawel with John Dille. Spy in the U.S. New York: Harper and Row, 1961.

X, et al. Double Eagle: The Autobiography of a Polish Spy Who Defected to the West. Indianapolis: Bobbs-Merrill Company, 1979.

Russia/USSR

Agabekov, George. OGPU: The Russian Secret Terror. New York: Brentano's, 1931.

Barron, John. KGB: The Secret Work of Soviet Secret Agents. New York: Reader's Digest Press, 1974.

Boyle, Andrew. The Fourth Man: The Definitive Account of Kim Philby, Guy Burgess, and Donald Maclean and Who Recruited Them to Spy for Russia. New York: Dial Press, 1979.

Central Intelligence Agency. Counterintelligence Staff. The Rote Kapelle: The CIA's History of Soviet Intelligence and Espionage Networks in Western Europe, 1936-1945. Washington: University Publications of America, Inc., 1979.

Dallin, David J. Soviet Espionage. New Haven, CT: Yale University Press, 1955.

Deriabin, Peter and Gibney, Frank. The Secret World. Garden City, NY: Doubleday, 1959.

_____. Watchdogs of Terror: Russian Bodyguards from the Tsars to the Commissars. New Rochelle, NY: Arlington House, 1972.

Foote, Alexander. Handbook for Spies. Garden City, NY: Doubleday, 1949.

Hingley, Ronald. The Russian Secret Police: Muscovite, Imperial Russian and Soviet Political Security Operations. New York: Simon and Schuster, 1970.

121

Khokhlov, Nikolai Y. In the Name of Conscience: The Testament of a Soviet Secret Agent. New York: David McKay Company, 1959.

Myagkov, Aleksei. Inside the KGB: An Expose by an Officer of the Third Directorate. New Rochelle, NY: Arlington House, 1977.

Penkovskiy, Oleg. The Penkovskiy Papers. Garden City, NY: Doubleday, 1965.

Philby, Harold Adrian Russell ("Kim"). My Silent War. New York: Grove Press, 1968.

Sakharov, Vladimir and Tosi, Umberto. High Treason. New York: G.P. Putnam's Sons, 1980.

Seale, Patrick and McConville, Maureen. Philby: The Long Road to Moscow. New York: Simon and Schuster, 1973.

Sigl, Rupert. In the Claws of the KGB: Memoirs of a Double Agent. Ardmore, PA: Dorrance & Company, 1978.

Trevor-Roper, Hugh. The Philby Affair. London: Kimber, 1968.

Whiteside, Thomas. An Agent in Place: The Wennerstrom Affair. New York: Viking Press, 1966.

Wittlin, Thaddeus. Commissar: The Life and Death of Lavrenty Pavlovich Beria. New York: Macmillan, 1972.

Wolin, Simon and Slusser, Robert M., editors. The Soviet Secret Police. Westport, CT: Greenwood Press, 1964.

Government Scrutiny

The following three groups investigated the U.S. intelligence community in 1975. They held numerous hearings and published those hearings plus other reports.

U.S. Commission on CIA Activities Within the United States. Report to the President. Washington: U.S. Government Printing Office, June, 1975.

U.S. Congress. House. Select Committee on Intelligence. Recommendations of the Final Report of the House Select Committee on Intelligence. Washington: U.S. Government Printing Office, 1976.

_____. Hearings. Washington: U.S. Government Printing Office, 1976.

U.S. Congress. Senate. Select Committee to Study Governmental
Operations with Respect to Intelligence Activities. Final
Report. Washington: U.S. Government Printing Office, 1976.

_____. Hearings. Washington: U.S. Government Printing
Office, 1976.

Two permanent congressional committees conduct ongoing review
and oversight of the intelligence community. They publish reports
and hearings periodically and on an ad hoc basis.

U.S. Congress. House. Permanent Select Committee on Intelligence.

U.S. Congress. Senate. Select Committee on Intelligence.

Bibliographies and Encyclopedias

Blackstock, Paul W. and Schaf, Frank L., Jr. Intelligence,
Espionage, Counterespionage, and Covert Operations: A Guide
to Information Sources. Detroit: Gale Research Company,
1978.

Buncher, Judith F., et al, eds. The CIA and the Security Debate:
1971-1975. New York: Facts on File, 1976.

Buranelli, Vincent and Buranelli, Nan. Spy/Counterspy: An Encyclopedia of Espionage. New York: McGraw-Hill Company, Inc.,
1982.

Defense Intelligence School. Bibliography of Intelligence Litera-
ture: A Critical and Annotated Bibliography of Open-Source
Literature. 7th edition (revised). Washington: Defense
Intelligence School, 1981.

Fain, Tyrus G., Katherine C. Plant, and Ross Milroy. The Intelligence Community: History, Organization and Issues. New
York: R.R. Bowker Company, 1977.

Seth, Ronald. Encyclopedia of Espionage. 2nd edition. Garden
City, NY: Doubleday and Company, Inc., 1975.

WESTMAR COLLEGE LIBRARY